WATSON

For rights and permissions, please contact:
Parchment & Forge, LLC
1942 Broadway St. STE 314C
Boulder CO 80302

Cover design by Katarina Naskovski
Formatted by Bodie Dykstra

ISBN: 979-8-9909-0120-9 (eBook)
ISBN: 979-8-9909012-1-6 (Soft Cover)
ISBN: 979-8-9909012-2-3 (Hard Cover)

To Watson, may we carry on your legacy.

PERSONAL MEMOIRS OF A CIVIL WAR PIONEER

WATSON

WATSON STEWART

PUBLISHER'S PREFACE

The existence of a collection of memoirs from Watson Stewart was brought to my attention in 2023, by my Aunt—Ponna *Stewart* Logan—a result of much genealogical effort by the living Stewarts of the day (Alex Stewart, in particular). The original 1904 manuscript is an uninterrupted 63-page document, which has been subsequently divided—for this publication—into a set of chapters to assist in the approachability and navigation of the narrative. All other changes are minor in nature, as we have done everything in our power to maintain the historical integrity of Watson's original manuscript.

In this genealogical line, I find myself five generations removed from Watson. My mother, Leslie *Stewart* Sloan, along with Ponna *Stewart* Logan and Alex Stewart, are the children of Robert "Bob" Stewart. Robert is the son of Glenn Duncan Stewart, he being the son of Charles A Stewart, who is the son of Capt. Samuel J Stewart. Samuel—mentioned extensively in these memoirs—is the brother of Watson Stewart.

For those so inclined, most of the locations noted in these memoirs, such as the areas of Cottage Grove and Vegetarian Creek are with us, waiting to be visited in Southeastern Kansas. The Stone House built by Watson and Samuel can still be seen West of the Sad Saga of Vegetarian Creek Historical Marker.

One would also be remiss not to mention the efforts of the Kansas Collection Articles (and contributor Mitzi Bateman), which performed a great service by maintaining a version of these memoirs in its archives. This organization strives to let the voices of the past be heard through nearly-lost books, letters, diaries, photographs, and other materials.

My goal in publishing these memoirs is to continue that quest, and inspire others to carry on the tradition of posterity for their own familial lines. I hope you enjoy reading these memoirs as much as I enjoyed putting them together, and that they transport you to a time when our ancestors forged the paths that brought us all to the present.

Jeffrey William Sloan
May 27th, 2024 (Memorial Day)

PREFACE

For the past two years, I have, during my leisure time, compiled the following personal memoirs, with a view of putting into permanent form such a record of the principal events of my life, as would be of interest to my immediate family.

I cannot claim for the work, any literary merit. I have sought only to give a "plain, unvarnished tale", as to myself and my ancestors, in the hope that it will possess some interest to those for whom it is written.

I have been careful to state with accuracy, the facts given, as to persons and dates.

My inability to trace the genealogy of the family of "S T E W A R T" farther back than to my grandfather is a matter of regret to me.

A Mr. Watson Stewart, of Normal, Illinois, has placed me under obligations for information as to the ancestors of his family—showing strong marks of similarity to our branch of the family—evidencing the fact that both families are descended from the same ancestors.

I have not spoken at any length of my sons and their families; suffice it to say that, as to my wife and myself—if there has been one thing above another, in which we have prided ourselves, and of which we have boasted—it has been the fact that we were the parents of seven sons; all leading honorable, useful lives; all having reached manhood—some, middle life—all having brought into the family, wives whom we were proud to accept as daughters—and to have and love as such.

Cherishing these convictions and beliefs, a fond mother passed from this to a better life, a few years ago.

To the father, it has come to grieve over the wrongdoing of one. He rests in the hope, however, that the erring one may return, and, so far as possible, make amends for the wrongs done—to himself and friends; showing himself still worth of the name of Stewart.

* * * * * * * * * * * * * * *

Davenport Ia.

February 25, 1904

(77th birthday)

Watson Stewart

CHAPTER 1
OF THE FAMILY STEWART

I was born on a small farm in Miami County, Ohio, Feb. 25, 1827. My father was Joseph Stewart, my mother's name was Mary; her maiden name was Coe. I was the first born. My father was the first born of a large family of children; his father's name was Samuel; his mother's name was Sarah Buffington, before marriage.

My father was born in South Carolina, April 15, 1801. When only two or three years of age, with his parents, he came to Ohio.

My mother was the daughter of Joseph and Elizabeth Coe, and was born in Ohio, Dec. 17, 1806. I do not know much of my mother's family; but she was a daughter by second marriage of my grandfather, and of the third marriage of my grandmother.

My grandmother's maiden name was Parks; she first married a Carter, who was killed by the Indians; her second husband was a Cox, and he was thrown from a horse and killed; after which, she was married to Joseph Coe, my grandfather.

My mother and one sister were the only children born of that marriage, her sister dying young.

From the best information I have been able to obtain, my mother's parents came from Pennsylvania or New Jersey, to Ohio; settling near Cincinnati, but finally coming to Miami County about the year 1799.

The family of Stewarts are of Scotch-Irish descent, and, from the best information I have, three brothers came to this country, two of them settling in the North, and one in South Carolina; and from this one our family is descended.

My grandfather, early in the nineteenth century, removed to Shelby County, Ohio with his family. Here the family continued to reside until about 1838. When my grandfather, grandmother, and several of the younger children removed to Piatt County, Illinois.

There were, in the family, nine sons and one daughter who lived to mature years; two sons died in infancy.

The names of the family, in the order of birth, were Joseph, Hannah, John, Richard, Daniel, William, Myhew, Levi, Allen and Fielding W.

I am not able to give much definite information as to my ancestors; my father died when I was yet too young to have learned much from him, and for many years thereafter I took no interest in the matter, and when, in later years, I would gladly have learned more, the family were mostly removed to distant parts of the country, or were dead; and for a number of years past, no member of my father's family has been living.

While at El Reno, Oklahoma, in the summer of 1901, I learned that a man was there from Normal, Illinois, having my own name. I opened a correspondence with him, from which I am led to believe that our families came from the same ancestors. I quote from a letter of his, some facts as to his own family:

"My father was born in Butler Co., Pennsylvania, in 1799, and died at Normal, Illinois, in 1863; his name was Joseph Stewart. He moved with his parents to Harrison Co., Ohio, when he was a small boy, and lived there until 1854, when he moved to this place, (Norman). His father's name was John Stewart, born in the United States, but of Scotch descent; his mother's name was Mary Bell, also of Scotch descent. They had eight children, Elizabeth,

Samuel Watson, John, William, Jane, and Joseph—two others died in infancy."

Samuel Watson—after whom I was named—was married and had three children, John, Mary Ann, and William.

The following bit of family history may not be uninteresting to you, as it is authentic:

The Stewarts are of Norman blood; a Norman gentleman by the name of Alan accompanied William the Conqueror from Normandy into England, and obtained, by his gift, the lands and castles of Oswestry, in Shropshire. His eldest son, William, became the ancestor of the Earls of Arundel; the second son, Walter, went to Scotland and became prominent in the service of David I, and had large territory in possession; conferred upon him by that monarch, including the Barony of Renfrew, together with the office of Lord High Steward of Scotland.

The Stewardship became hereditary in his family, and was assumed by his descendants, (dropping their Norman name "Alan") as surname, with the single change of the final letter "d" to "t", so that the proper spelling of the name is not Stuart, but Stewart.

Mary, Queen of Scots, is responsible for the change of the spelling of the name, as she was educated in France, and that was their way of spelling it—Stuart. Her father, James V, spelled his name "Stewart" and his son, James VI did the same.

Walter Stewart was the name of the sixth Lord High Steward of Scotland; he greatly distinguished himself in the service of the reigning monarch, Robert Bruce, and married his daughter, Marjory, which alliance brought the crown of Scotland to his family.

Thus originated the "House of Stewart". Annie Stewart, best known as Queen Annie, daughter of James II, left no heirs, and on the theory then adopted, that the blood of James II—her father—had been corrupted in the direct line, it was decided by parliament that the nearest heir to the throne of England, in the line of the "Stewarts" was the son of the Erector (sic) of Brunswick, and of his wife Sophia, who was the daughter of James VI, of Scotland, and I, of England.

He was placed on the throne of England with the title of George I.

From him, Queen Victoria is a lineal descendant. She occupies the throne on account of her Stewart blood. And, referring back to Walter—surely, we can see how our own name, "Watson", was formed; as "Johnson" was given to a son of "John", "Smithson" to a son of "Smith" so, "Watson" was a son of "Walter" or "Wat".

From the foregoing, it seems probable that this family of Stewarts were the descendants of one of the three brothers coming to this country—probably in the early part of the 18th century, and who had settled in Pennsylvania.

The names are peculiarly the same, in many cases; and the name "Watson", in that family suggests the probability that our family—2— had knowledge of that branch; as I never knew of the name in our family, prior to my time. I never knew for whom I was named.

My father owned a small farm on the Miami river, between Troy and Piqua; was part owner of a water-mill; he was also a physician; and as I remember, he had an extensive country practice, and was very successful.

My mother died when I was only about eight years old, my memory of her, is that of a woman of slender build—rather tall, dark hair and eyes, and in delicate health—always patient with her children, and with strong religious feelings.

One of my most vivid recollections of her, was in connection with her desire to attend the church of which she was a member, to hear a favorite minister, in the early summer before her death; in which connection I was sent to build a fire in the church—distant about one mile from our house; it was her last attendance; she was wasting away with consumption, of which she died, soon after.

The church was a country church, of the "Christian", or "New

Light" sect; known as the "Rocky Springs Church"; as it was commonly spoken of.

Dying, my mother left four children; myself, Sarah, Elizabeth and Samuel.

Grandfather and grandmother Coe, lived in a small brick house in the same yard with us; our family lived in a large hewed log house, in fact, as I understand, my father built the brick house, when he was first married; and as the family increased, and it became necessary to have more room, an exchange of houses was made.

My father, some time after mother's death, married a widow—Garland; her husband and, I think, two children, having died. She was the daughter of Henry Hyatt, who lived in a small village south of Troy, named Hyattsville; they were English. My stepmother having been born in England, coming to this country when only a small child; her name was Ann. She came into the family of four small children, and it is a great pleasure for me to say, that she proved herself a good mother. Afterward, two children were born, Mary Ann and William; and we all lived together in perfect accord and harmony.

My Father, as I think of him, must have been a man of more than ordinary intelligence, in that day. And I think he was a radical in his views on all matters in thought and action affecting the people of that period. In religion, he was a member of the Christian or "New Light" church; which, in the early thirties was rent asunder by the teachings of Alexander Campbell; and he went off with that sect known as "Campbellites."

The "New Lights" laid great stress on the matter of "feeling" in religion, and were often wrought up to a perfect frenzy in feeling; sometimes were taken with what was known as the "jerks", in which the limbs of the body would become uncontrollable; and the person would be thrown upon the floor in an exhausted condition; others would jump and shout until, unable to stand, they would fall and lie in a comatose condition for hours at a time.

The "Campbellite" branch, laid more stress upon a strict compliance with the commands of the new Testament, and considered baptism by immersion as a very clear command, and essential to church membership. Both branches were Unitarian in belief.

In politics, my Father was a Democrat; but a radical Anti Slavery man; taking an active part in the agitation of the question, in public discussions, in vogue at that time; on some occasions being met by the opposition, in the use of stale eggs—a very common argument of those times.

He was also an earnest advocate of Temperance, being a total abstainer from the use of intoxicants; which, in his day, was a rare thing; as it was almost the universal custom for people to keep liquors in their houses, and use them daily; and it was almost impossible for farmers to get work done in harvest fields, unless liquor was furnished. I remember that both my father, and grandfather Coe, refused to furnish it, and they were sometimes put to great inconvenience in getting "hands" to work.

My father was also a reformer, in the practice of medicine; practicing the "Thompsonian System"; discarding the use of Calomel and other minerals, and the use of the lance in blood-letting, so common in those days; using, in lieu, vegetable remedies, cold and hot baths, etc. So, in looking back at these characteristics of the man, I conclude him to have been a progressive and advance thinker, of his day.

I was too young during his life to have noticed, particularly, these evidences of a reformer. I remember that he was popular, as a debater on these several questions. He was also greatly interested in educational matters.

He died when I was but thirteen years old; he had given me the best available opportunities to secure and maintain an education, but I only enjoyed the benefit of a three-months term of school, each winter, with a course of lessons in Kirkham's Grammar, given at our own house; with the addition of a few lessons in penmanship at a night school.

My father died Feb. 9, 1840, leaving six children to the care of a step-mother, as to four of us, of whom I was the oldest.

My services were required at home, so that, for about two years I could not go to school; then I went for one term of three months; and this completed my education, as far as schools were concerned.

My father, about two years prior to his death, had built a two-story frame dwelling house, in the building of which I think, he became some-what involved in debt; so that in the settling up of his estate, there was very little left, after the debts were paid.

We continued on the farm for about two years; most of the work de-volving upon me; my sisters often lending a helping hand—as they could. Our farm, in connection with grandfather's, only contained about sixty acres, lying on the east bank of the Miami River and north of Spring creek; it was fenced into four or five fields, and had three acres in sugar maple trees, from which, every spring, we made our supply of sugar and syrup.

We had the three houses in which our family and grandfather Coe lived; and two other houses, in which families of the mill men lived; an old orchard of very large apple trees; and on the east side, an old family, and neighborhood burying ground; where lie my mother, father and their youngest son, who died in infancy; also, grandfather and grandmother Coe, who had both died within two years of the death of my father. And now, as I look back for more than sixty years, it all comes back to me as clearly as the happenings and scenes of yesterday. But time has wrought great changes.

I visited the old place in 1895, and while the lay of the land and the river had a familiar look, not a vestige of the old mill, residences or or-chard, remains; the farm has passed into the possession of a party own-ing adjoining land, and all buildings had been removed.

My stepmother, after about two years of widowhood, married one J. C. Winans, quite a prominent man, owning a farm on Spring Creek about one mile east of our place; and a former partner with my father in the mill business. He had a family of four children; and with them we went to live; making a family of ten children when all were at home. My brother Samuel, about this time, went to live with his uncle William, in Champaign County, Ill., and my sister Sarah, for much of the time, lived with my stepmother's sister, Mrs. Favorite, in Tippecanoe. Thus, our old home was broken up, and in my sixteenth year, I set out to make my own way.

CHAPTER 2
OF EARLY ADVENTURES

I worked about one year on the farm, for Mr. Winans, my Stepmother's husband. I was paid five dollars per month, with board, washing and mending. Mr. Winans was running a tomb-stone shop on his farm; a workman, by the name of J. D. Brant, was running the shop. He was a man past the middle age, a good workman, much addicted to strong drink, and quite a politician, of the Democratic stamp, had a violent temper, quickly aroused in political discussions.

I concluded to learn the trade; and spent three years as an apprentice under Mr. Brant; receiving, as wages, fifty dollars per annum, with board and washing, as before.

During these years, a son of the boss, J. J. Brant, was a fellow apprentice. He was about two years my senior in age; he and I became warm friends, which friendship continued for many years thereafter. During these years of apprenticeship, my chum Brant and I read all that we could get hold of on phrenology and mesmerism; especially the works published by Fowler & Wells, of New York; also took courses of instruction from traveling lecturers; and we went so far as to buy out an outfit from one "Professor" Kid, a very interesting lecturer on Phrenology. This outfit consisted of a number of life-sized pictures of celebrated characters, and others illustrating the different temperaments, etc. Also, skulls and plaster casts, and a galvanic battery; the battery, at that time, was quite a novelty, and served to amuse an audience.

After practicing for awhile in the neighborhood school-houses in the country, we came to believe that we could make a success in other fields; and only awaited the accumulation of sufficient funds to make a start.

During the time I was learning my trade, was a formative period of my life in opinion on many matters, influencing my character for life. In politics, I had been reared a Democrat, but I soon came to accept the theory of the Whig party, on the protective tariff.

At that time, there was very little manufacturing in this country; nearly all our wool and cotton goods were imported from England, and it was a favorite method of the Whig speaker, in a political meeting, to wear, and exhibit a suit of clothes of American manufacture; thus showing that such goods could be made in our own country; and, if so, then it was a good policy for us to encourage their manufacture by a tariff on foreign goods, imported into this country. Henry Clay was notably a leading champion of this policy.

The question of slavery, and especially of its extension into our new territories, was beginning to occupy a very prominent place in the politics of the country; and I, very early took sides, with the Anti-Slavery party, by whatever name it was known; and, as both the Democratic and Whig parties vied with each other in their subserviency to the Slave power, I never voted with either party.

My first vote for President was for John P. Hale, in 1852, a candidate of the "Free Democratic" party. I also early espoused the Temperance cause, becoming a member of the "Sons of Temperance" at about the age of eighteen.

As to religion, I had been, all my life, under the influence of strictly orthodox religious teaching; my father and mother, grandfather and grandmother Coe, and nearly all my relatives, were members of the Christian, or "New Light" church, known as the "Rocky Springs" church, situated about a mile from our home, on the Miami river; and while my parents lived, our house was the home for preachers and others, attending what was called "Big Meetings", held about once a year, and usually holding a week or more.

At about seventeen years of age, I united with this church, fully accepting all their doctrines. I was, however, always disposed to read such discussions as came in my way, on religious subjects, and about this time I read a very able debate held in Cincinnati, Ohio, between Rev. Mr. Rice, a Presbyterian minister of that city, and a Mr. Pingree of Louisville, Ky., a minister of the Universalist church. The reading of the arguments as presented by these very able disputants, somewhat unsettled my belief in the future everlasting punishment of a portion of the human family; and a further consideration of the questions under all available light from Scripture, science and reason, soon led me to accept the comfortable belief in the "Fatherhood of God", and the "Brotherhood of Man"; and I settled down to the conviction that such a relationship would ultimate somehow, and at some time, in the happiness of all the human family; and in that conviction, I have ever after rested; being fully convinced that an all-wise, omnipotent and loving father, could never have created one of his children to be consigned to eternal torment.

With these opinions and beliefs, I had adopted certain views at that time considered very radical by most persons, and by many, quite heterodox, as, for instance, I adopted the vegetarian diet. I also eschewed tea and coffee, discarded the use of medicine, and practiced the water-cure system in disease; I favored women's suffrage, and was favorably inclined toward Socialism as it is generally understood.

In later life, I somewhat modified my views on these several questions; coming to believe that for the most part, they are, in themselves, right, but as Society is at present constituted, they are not practicable.

In the fall of 1845, my chum Brant and I, planned a trip to Illinois, as he had some relatives in Christian county, and I had some in Pyatt and Champaign counties. We therefore thought of buying a light wagon, each furnishing a horse, and starting overland on the trip; a distance of three or four hundred miles, over a country for much of the way but sparsely settled, and some very bad roads; but in the end we reached our destination without serious mishap.

It was my purpose, after a visit of a month or so, to return to Ohio horseback. At that time, there was not a railroad on the route, indeed, I think there was not one in Illinois, and only one in Indiana—a line from Madison, on the Ohio river, to Indianapolis. My brother Samuel was living with his Uncle William; my grandmother Stewart was living there, and several uncles, and my father's only sister, Aunt Hannah Moore. They were all living along the Sangamon river, in the counties of Pyatt and Champaign.

Urbana, a small village, was the County seat of Champaign; and Monticello, a new and very small place, the county seat of Pyatt. From the settlement on the river, to Urbana, 12 miles, there was but one house, and where the city of Champaign now is, was unentered government land.

After making a very pleasant visit with my friends, I was urged to remain all winter and teach a country school; and while I was not yet twenty years old, and, in my own judgment, but poorly qualified for the task, I consented, passed the necessary examination, receiving a certificate, and was duly installed as the teacher of a three-months school, at a salary of $55.00 for the term. The school house had been built of logs, with a large fireplace in one end; there were no pupils far advanced, and, for the most part, they were of a very low grade; some young men and girls who were older than the teacher, could only read in the "first reader".

I succeeded in giving general satisfaction, getting along with but little trouble, and enjoyed the roughness of it very much; none of my relatives lived near enough for me to board with them, so I secured board with a family nearby from Monday mornings till Friday nights, when I went to my Uncle's for Saturday and Sunday.

I was noted as a great lover of corn-bread, and at my boarding place, I got almost of surfeit of it, as we never had any other kind during my stay with them.

I met some odd characters during that winter; some rough, but generally kind and hospitable; one man, I especially remember, who was a preacher of the Christian, or "Campbellite" church—preaching nearly every Sunday, and during the week running a small distillery.

He was past middle age, with little education, but well-read in the Scriptures, and a ready talker. I don't think that he drank to excess, himself, but he thought it all right to make it and use it as one of the "God-given creature comforts of life."

In the spring of 1846, I started back to Ohio on horse-back.

I don't remember how long I was on the road, but probably nearly a month, as I went out of my way to visit an uncle John Stewart and family who lived near Wabash, Indiana. I finally reached home after a ride I think, of about 400 miles.

I struck the Wabash river at Covington, and traveled up that stream through Attica, Lafayette, Delphi and Logansport, to Wabash.

At that time, the canal was building from Toledo, to Evansville, Indiana.

From Wabash, I pursued an easterly course through Indiana, passing over a heavily wooded country, but sparsely settled; much of the way over what was called "corduroy" roads—built by lying logs across the roadway, side by side, usually on wet or marshy land.

During the summer of 1846, I worked at the stone-cutter's trade for Mr. Winans, at $40.00 per month. By that autumn, my friend Brant and I thought that we were well enough equipped to start on our lecture tour on Phrenology, Mesmerism, and kindred subjects; and, after giving a few lectures in the school houses in our neighborhood, we made our start. We gathered such funds as we could secure—I think, less than $100.00—and went first to Cincinnati, where we laid in a small supply of books, in line with our proposed lectures, with a view to selling them as we traveled.

From Cincinnati we struck out through Indiana in a northern and westerly course, stopping at the smaller towns, where we would put up at a hotel, put out advertising for two or three lectures at night; and during the days, at the hotels, we would give Phrenological examinations with a chart if desired. Our lectures were generally free, as the means of advertising ourselves; but sometimes we charged a small admission at the door. Our hall would be pretty well supplied with our large pictures hung upon the walls; on our stand, we exhibited two or three human skulls and plaster-casts, and the galvanic battery.

One of us would usually give a lecture on Phrenology, lasting about half an hour, after which a few Phrenological examinations would be made and some Mesmeric experiments given, and shocks with the galvanic battery would close the entertainment.

It was not difficult to fill out an evening's entertainment in a satisfactory manner. Such an enterprise may seem to have been wholly impracticable, and doomed to certain failure.

I was but twenty years old and Brant was but about two years older.

But I now believe, after all these years, that if we had owned our conveyance, and possessed a little more assurance and persistence, we might have succeeded. At that time, the subject of Phrenology was attracting very general attention; and experiments in Mesmerism were novel and interesting. Brant was possessed of more confidence than I, but either of us could put in more than an hour, with our lecture in connection with our mesmeric experiments, battery, etc., to the satisfaction of an audience. We, however, after about two months of effort concluded that if we could find work at our trade, we would do so, at least for a time; give up our enterprise, and, in fact, we were the more readily lead to this conclusion by the fact that our funds were running low; our expense of travel from place to place, was too great for our income.

We were getting up into the state, towards Lafayette, where Brant, on his return the year before from Illinois, had stopped and worked for a short time; and we therefore went there, hoping to get work for the winter, at least.

But it so happened that, just then, the shops were supplied with all the hands required. We learned, however, that a man by the name of Killen, was running a shop on his farm, about twenty fives miles down the river and about three miles from Attica, a pretty good town in Fountain county, and that he was in need of one or two men. Now we had felt quite sure of getting work in Lafayette, and our funds were running very low— so low, in fact, that we were not justified in paying a hotel bill there for a single night's lodging; so, finding a canal boat going out that night, we took passage, reaching Attica sometime after midnight; it was dark, the streets were not lighted; we were in a strange place, were not sure of getting work, but could not go further, as our funds, after paying our fare on the boat, were reduced to just seventy five cents, all told. However, we found a hotel, got a bed, and in the morning had our breakfast; then we held a consultation as to our future actions. We had our outfit; some books unsold, and our clothing; and we concluded that I should remain at the hotel, while Brant should walk out the three miles to see if we could get work; and, that he might make as good an impression as possible, we spent our seventy five cents for a new shirt for him to wear, our supply was in an unlaundered condition. He went out, returning in the afternoon, with the joyful news that we could get a job for all winter at $40.00 per month, each, with board.

And right here, it has always appeared to me, was the crisis, the turning point, in my life; by what seemed a mere chance, a thing happened without forethought on my part; until the day before, by which I found myself stranded here, and by a seeming chance obtained a footing from which my whole life course was determined.

Of course, we felt that fortune was setting in our favor.

We left our baggage at the hotel as security for our bill, and walked out the next morning and went to work. We found Mr. Killen a very pleasant man to work for; he owned a stone quarry from which he obtained stone for building purposes, and also worked into tomb-stone's using some marble, also. The native stone was a sandstone. He employed two or three other men in the quarry and mainly to do the engraving of tombstones. We worked here for more than a year, with very little loss of time, and saved most of our wages; as our opportunities for spending money were limited, living as we did in the country, seldom going to town; on Sunday we generally attended a country church, Methodist, called "Bethel" about one mile from our place of work.

Mr. Killen was a local Methodist preacher, and a man of much more than ordinary intelligence; a great reader, and a close reasoner in an argument. However, he was not dogmatic or bigoted but quite inclined to look for, and accept the truth, when found.

Our shop was a large log house, with a fireplace in one end; in the other end, we had our sleeping place, and in this shop we spent the greater part of both our days and nights; and it became a sort of meeting place for some of the nearby neighbormen and our boys, during the long winter nights; and it became a sort of meeting place for some of the near by debaters, also. We set apart one night of each week for the debate of some question of interest, and had some very good discussions.

Of our own force, we had our employer, Mr. Killen, ourselves and a very bright Irishman named Mullen; among the neighbors joining with us, was notably a Mr. Rhodes, a man living near by, and engaged in running a small wood turning shop, who showed considerable ability in our discussions.

Years after, in Kansas, he was the presiding Elder of the Emporia M. E. District. I never met him in Kansas, but he stood quite high in the church as a minister.

On the whole, the time I spent here was one of the most enjoyable of my life. Here I fell in with C. H. Grosvenor, a young man from Troy, Ohio; a town near my birthplace; he was not an engraver on stone, only a dresser of building stone; he married here, a twin girl by the name of Campbell; he afterwards became my business partner in Lafayette. Brant also found his wife there, a handsome girl named Lyon.

In the winter of 1847, I went to Attica to operate a marble shop for Mr. Killen. I remained in charge of this shop for about a year, doing a fairly good business.

In the Fall of 1848, I returned on a visit to my old home in Ohio; I was there during the Presidential election, but I had lost my citizenship by an absence of more than a year. Could I have voted, my vote would have been cast for the nominee of the "Free Soil" party, Martin Van Buren. Both of the old parties, in their platforms, had declared against the agitation of the slavery question.

CHAPTER 3
OF MARBLE AND MARRIAGE

On my return to Indiana, I went to Cincinnati by canal, on river boat from there to Madison, thence to Indianapolis by railroad; and from there by stage coach to Lafayette, and from there about twenty five miles to destination, I walked. I may say, in this connection, that at that time there were no railroads in that part of Ohio, and the only railroads. In Indiana was the one on which I traveled from Madison to Indianapolis, the rails of which were flat bars; Ohio had a canal from Toledo to Cincinnati, and Indiana had one from Toledo to Evansville.

In the Spring of 1849, I was offered a place in Lafayette.

There were two shops there; one run by a Mr. Berryhill, and the other by a Mr. Clark. I had all the time had a desire to go there; and I dissolved my very pleasant relations with Mr. Killen, and accepted the offer made by Mr. Clark, the more readily in that he offered me an increase in wages of $10.00 per month.

Mr. Clark was running quite a force of men in the shop, while he spent the greater part of his time in making the delivery of the work to the country; and I was put in charge of the force in the shop. He soon concluded to adopt a rather unique method of doing business; heretofore, an agent had been sent out to take contracts for such work as was agreed upon, and the work would be done in the shop and delivered as per contract; but he would fill his wagon with an assorted lot of stones, ready for lettering, and drive down the road from house to house; and, on selling a stone, it would be left; and thus he would go on until the load was disposed of.

He wished me to take the list of these sales, and go from house to house and finish up the work of lettering them as per agreement; and, as an inducement, he proposed to pay me $2.00 per day, furnish a horse for me to ride, and pay all my expenses, which was better wages than was paid any other employee; and, as I was a single man, and could about as well be in one place as another, I took the job. He furnished me a horse, and I took along such tools as I would need. The work was done all under many difficulties; I would call at the place where the work was to be done, would find the stone was in some outhouse, or, possibly, under the bed; and I would have to improvise some place on which to lay the stone, that I might do the work; generally, I would have it on a table in the dining or some other room in the house, with from one to half a dozen children, all curious to see the work as it was being done; and, in fact, the older members of the family were greatly interested in watching the process of engraving letters in stone; it seems to most persons, a very wonderful accomplishment, to be able to do such work.

Under such conditions and surroundings, it was somewhat difficult to do the work; at the same time, it gave me the opportunity of seeing and conversing with all kinds of people, some pleasant and entertaining, and some otherwise.

On the whole, I rather liked the business. Sometimes, I would be out two or three weeks on a trip; often having to travel several miles from place to place, and the entire trip extending into two or more counties.

Mr. Clark was an active, pushing man, of the most abstemious Habits; but he was not successful, in a business way. He seemed always to be in debt, but I had the fullest confidence in his honesty, and I worked through the winter of 1848-49, and up to the middle of the next summer, only drawing as much of my wages as was needed; so that, at the end of that time, he was in my debt about $300.00. My friend Grosvenor, had also, in the meantime, come to work for Mr. Clark.

Lafayette was at that time a thriving place, with a population of about 8,000. At times of high water in Wabash, Steamboats came up the river to this point; but the principal shipping business was done on the canal. It had no railroads at that date; in two or three years, it had two; the "New Albany & Salem", and the "Lafayette & Indianapolis."

During the summer of 1849, the cholera visited Lafayette, assuming a malignant form. Business utterly collapsed, and for about six weeks remained so; nearly half of the population fled from the city, and yet, out of the reduced number remaining, when at its worst stage, as many as from fifteen to seventeen deaths occurred in a day. The city took on a funeral appearance; no business doing, except that connected with the care of the sick, and burying the dead. The town was shunned by all the outside world.

Both Mr. Clark and Mr. Berryhill, the marble men of the place, were stricken down by the disease. I was with many cases of sickness and death; was with Mr. Clark until his death, yet I escaped an attack; but the experience was one that I trust I may never have again.

After the plague had left us, and we got on our feet again, and began to look about us, I found myself in quite a perplexing situation; both men who were running the business at which I had worked, were dead; and the wages which I had been saving up for several months, were, for the present at least, tied up.

H. W. Chase, a lawyer and personal friend of the Clark family was appointed administrator of the estate; and it was soon found that very little was left for either family or creditors. The family consisted of the widow and two daughters ages about 14 and 18 respectively. As I now remember, only about 10 percent of the unsecured debts were paid. Mr. Chase suggested to Mr. Grosvenor and me to take the stock of marble on hand; he proposing to furnish the funds to pay for it, and buy additional stock as needed; we forming a partnership under the name of "Stewart & Grosvenor"; he to be a silent partner in the business.

This seemed to us, a very fortunate scheme, and we accepted, with gladness, his offer. So, in the autumn of 1849, the firm of "Stewart & Grosvenor" was duly launched in the business world. The firm started out under very favorable conditions, neither Grosvenor nor I had much money to put into the business; we cheerfully put in our best efforts in labor and Mr. Chase furnished the capital.

During the fall, it became necessary for us to lay in additional stock of marble for the winter's use, and I was sent to Buffalo, N. Y., to make the purchase. Our stock, at that time, all came to us by water; on the lake to Toledo, and from there on the canal.

I traveled from Lafayette to Toledo on a canal boat, from there to Buffalo by lake steamer over Lake Erie. This was a new experience to me, and I was very sick on the lake; it being quite rough; but on arriving at my destination I was feeling all right; and after making the purchase of the marble, I took a day off from business for pleasure, and visited Niagara Falls. It impressed me, as it doubtless does all visitors, as wonderful and sublime beyond the power of human to describe.

On my return home, after a few days, I was taken violently sick with what the doctor at first called "bilious fever", but which, in a few days more, developed into a case of smallpox of a most virulent type. I was boarding with the family of my late employer—Mrs. Clark,—she was keeping several boarders; her own family, with the boarders, making eight or ten persons in all.

These people all having been exposed to the disease, before its character was known, were duly quarantined in the house, and I was shut up in a room away from the other occupants of the house. An Irish woman who had had the disease, was employed to come to my room each day and render such assistance as was necessary, in cleaning up the room, bringing me food, etc.

The doctor also came daily, and, for a time, twice a day; and for about a month these were the only persons coming into my room.

After the disease had run about ten days, I had a good appetite, but was not permitted to eat any rich or greasy food—as meat, butter, or milk. My rations consisted, mainly, of molasses and mush; also, dry toast, tea, and rice; but I relished my food. I came out in the end in good physical condition; in fact, feeling unusually well. Fortunately, the family and boarders, by being vaccinated, and confining themselves to plain diet, escaped with very light attacks of Varioloid. And the disease did not spread at all. In my own case, I was very fortunate in escaping with very slight markings. It was a rather severe stroke on me, financially, just at the commencement of my business, and among a people largely strangers. The doctor's and nurses' bills, loss of time, and also the necessary burning of all the bedding in my room, amounted to quite a sum; but I got through it all with the aid of very kind friends, found in connection with a Temperance society of which I was a member; the "Temple of Honor."

It was never known where I had been exposed to the disease; I never had, knowingly, come into contact with a case, but I had probably been exposed while on my trip east, by sleeping in some infected berth on the lake or the canal. My attack was not a light one, and I probably owe my recovery and freedom from pock marks to my vigorous physical health and temperate habits.

About this time I united with the "Christian", "Campbellite" church. While I was not in accord with all the doctrines of this church, the pastor, old father Longley, understood my position, and I found the members generally a very pleasant, social people, of liberal views.

The Temperance cause was, at this time, in Indiana, holding a very prominent place in the minds of the people. Among other organizations active in this cause, was the "Temple of Honor", a secret society with several degrees, using a very pretty ritual both in the lodge and in its degree work. I early became a member of this order, and in due time, having taken its several degrees, and having served as its W.C.T., Worthy Chief Templar, the presiding officer of the lodge, I was elected to the Grand Lodge of the state, and met with that body at Indianapolis, and at one session in Lafayette.

This order, for the encouragement of the lady workers in the cause, established a degree called the "Social Degree", in which only members of the Temple of Honor were eligible, and such ladies as might be elected to membership by the members of the degree.

The initiation ceremony of this degree was very beautiful and appropriate; its officers were all dual; one male and one female in each position. We had a very working order, both as to the Temple and the "Social Degree". My connection with this order brought me into the society of a very good class of people. To this order, no doubt, I owe the finding of my wife. I had not gone into society to any extent, and formed the acquaintance of but few ladies. It was in the Fall and winter of 1849-50, that, among the lady members of the Degree, I met Miss Elizabeth Tipton. She, as well as I, was a constant attendant on the weekly meetings of the lodge, and thus we were thrown much together in our work.

The "Social Degree" was also what is implied by its name, and we often had social entertainments given by its members in our hall, at which outside friends, by invitation, met with us for a good time socially. In course of time, she and I were elected as presiding officers, jointly, and, from that to the Grand Lodge of the State.

We were thus brought together in our work in the temperance cause and in our social relations and this resulted in our final union for life work; consummated by our marriage on October 30, 1851.

We were married by the Chaplain of our order, Reverend Barwick;

most of the friends present were members of the "Social Degree" Temple of Honor.

Elizabeth Tipton was the only daughter of Joshua and Cynthia Tipton, and was born in Cincinnati, Ohio, September 19, 1832; her father having died of cholera about two months before her birth; during its ravage of that city in that year. Mrs. Tipton continued to reside in that place until the daughter was about ten years old, when they removed to Lafayette, Indiana, near where she had two brothers residing; John and George Wilson. John was a well-to-do farmer with a family of five or six children, living about three miles east of Lafayette; George was an old bachelor.

This brings me along in my life to where I began to make a home for myself and wife. I was in my twenty-fifth year, my wife in her nineteenth. My business was fairly good, quite up to my expectations. The firm of "Stewart & Grosvenor" stood well in the community, and we were reaching far out for business; and our married life started under favorable conditions.

Our first born was a girl—born December 8, 1852, and we gave to her the name of "Cynthia."

Probably about the beginning of 1853, I bought out the interest of both Mr. Grosvenor and Mr. Chase, and continued the business in my own name.

The manner of soliciting business, in those days, was to send out agents over the country to take contracts for work to be delivered at a certain time as per contract; these agents were paid from 10 to 12 percent on the sales made; and the business was thus extended through several big counties—often for a distance of from 100 to 200 miles. On delivery of the work to the parties in interest, very generally, notes were taken in payment, running until the following Christmas, as that was the general "pay day" at that time.

If your agents were always honest and careful as to the persons to whom they sold, it was all right, but too often, in order to secure the commission on a sale, they would contract with a party wholly irresponsible; and thus, much was lost in that manner.

I call to mind one man of this kind, through whose sales I lost largely. His name was Saunders; a man of middle age, a smooth talker, but wholly unscrupulous. He claimed to be a preacher, and when out in the country took every occasion to so represent himself; attending all places of religious meetings and taking an active part in them, thus becoming acquainted with as many of the people as possible; if hearing of a death, he would make it a point to attend the funeral, and in a day or two afterward, he would call on the friends while they were in a tender mood, and get a contract for a tombstone for the deceased, if possible.

He would sell to any one, without any questions as to their ability to pay. He sold more stone than anyone else, and before I had an opportunity to learn his character, I was involved in a rather heavy loss. I am sure he was a consummate old scamp.

In the years of 1852-53, the "Know-nothing" move in politics almost disrupted the old parties. It sprang into being from a fear that the Catholics were getting into too great control for the government.

It was ostensibly an "American" party, seeking to restrict immigration, and put the control of the Government into the hands of Americans only; but its real fight was against the Catholic Church. They worked with great secrecy—meeting in secret—and running a man for office, and then voting for him solidly, so that, in some cases, both of the old parties having candidates contesting for the place, on election day, a person would be elected who had not been, in public, named for the office. I was not in sympathy with the objects of this party, but as I was wholly out of touch with both the old parties, I was induced to join them; but I never heartily espoused their cause, and seldom met with them. The party made a mushroom growth, and in a short time, as quickly, died out.

In 1854, the passage of the Kansas-Nebraska bill aroused the whole country on the question of the extension of Slavery into the Territories of the United States. The old Whig party became absorbed by the Anti-Slavery party. A state convention was held in Indianapolis in June 1854, composed of persons from all parties who were opposed to the extension of slavery. And here the Republican party had its inception, in the union of the Anti-slavery elements of the Democratic and Whig parties with the old "Free-Soil" party. I was a member of that convention. A similar convention was held in Columbus, Ohio, at the same time. And from this movement, set on foot at these conventions, the great Republican party was formed; and, with that party, I have ever since affiliated.

This was soon after the passage of the Kansas-Nebraska bill, and excitement ran high. John Pettit, of Lafayette, one of the Senators who had voted for the bill, and who, in the discussion of the measure, had said that the portion of the declaration of Independence, stating that "all men are created equal" was a "self-evident lie".

On returning home, and in attempting to justify his actions in a speech before a large audience in the court house, he was hooted down and was unable to make himself heard.

I think it was in 1854, that my brother Samuel came from Illinois to make his home with me, and assist me in the business, in doing such of the outside work, in selling and delivering stones, and making collections. He was about twenty one years of age.

On the 12th of February, a son was born, and we named him Frank.

During these several years of business life, nothing of unusual interest occurred; my business was fairly good, and yet I cherished a hope of sometime removing to the country and engaging in farming.

A great deal was written and said about the delightful climate, healthfulness and beauty of Kansas; and many efforts were put forth in the North to colonize the country by organizing companies of congenial people, who would settle together in communities. My brother and I read much that was published in the New York Tribune, and other papers, about the efforts being made in the Southern States, especially by Missouri, to overrun the territory, and establish slavery therein, and became much interested in the matter.

CHAPTER 4

OF THE SAD SAGA OF VEGETARIAN CREEK

During the summer of 1855, we learned of the formation of a company called the "Vegetarian Settlement Company", organized for the purpose of making a settlement in Kansas. Its officers were Charles H. DeWolf, of Philadelphia, President; John McLauren, Treasurer, and Henry S. Clubb, of New York, Secretary. The purpose and plan of operation of this company may be understood from the following extract from a circular issued by the officers, dated Dec. 1, 1855, in connection with a few articles of their constitution.

Art 2.

> *The Company shall be conducted on the mutual joint-stock principle, for the equal benefit of all the members, and to protect each other from the impositions of speculators and monopolists, by raising sufficient funds to start with efficient machinery, implements, and provisions.*

Art. 4

> *Persons of good moral character, who shall be approved by the board of directors, whether male or female, who are not slave-holders, may become members of the company, on paying $1.00 entrance fee, and an installment of 10 cents per share,*

on not less than twenty shares. Each member may subsequently purchase additional shares, no member, however, shall be allowed to hold more than 240 shares at any one time. Each person, on becoming a member must agree to sign the following declaration upon entering the settlement:

I . . . . do voluntarily agree to abstain from all intoxicating liquors as beverages, from tobacco in every form, and from the flesh of animals; promote social, moral, political freedom; to maintain the observance of all good and righteous laws, and to otherwise conform to the rules adopted by a majority of the Vegetarian Settlement Company.

The capital stock of the Company consisted of shares of from 65 up, each, equal in number to the acres of land located. The circular of December 1, 1855, referred to says in part:

"In September last, Dr. John McLauren, as one of the directors, proceeded to explore Kansas Territory, and after spending several weeks traveling along the Kansas, Osage, and other rivers, he came to the conclusion that a fine site on the Neosho river, between latitude 38 degrees and the boundary line of the Osage Indian lands, and between 18 and 19 degrees longitude west from Washington, would be the best location for the Vegetarian settlement. He accordingly took possession of a claim, comprising excellent water privileges. The Neosho river, at this point is very rapid, and for ten months in the year, the water is sufficiently abundant to make it serviceable for mill power. It is free from any bad taste, and is very soft. There is sufficient amount of timber to serve the purposes of Settlers until additional timber can be grown. Coal, limestone and sandstone, suitable for grindstones, etc., and abundant springs of pure water, are interspersed throughout a fine rolling prairie; and

the land comprises an excellent vegetable mold, loam, etc., to great
depth, with a gravely, and, in some instances, rocky substratum.
The scenery is beautiful, and the surface undulating like the waves
of the ocean subsiding after a storm. The banks of the river are from
15 to 30 feet high, so that a milldam can be easily constructed with-
out causing an overflow. Altogether, it does not appear that a more
suitable site could be found for the purposes of the Company."

The aim of this company, and its plan of operations, as set forth, seemed
feasible; and in accord with our views. And from what we learned of
the promoters through the New York Tribune, and the "Phrenological
Journal", my brother and I took stock in it, and at once began prepara-
tions to go with the company to Kansas.

In the early spring of 1855, I sold out my business to John W. Pampell.
We had a wagon made to order, bought a team of fine young horses, and,
early in March my brother started overland with wagon, team, and outfit for camping. It was his purpose to drive to St. Louis and there meet
with other members of the company, and together to proceed overland to
Kansas. He was then to return to Jefferson City, Mo., where myself and
family (having journeyed thus far by public conveyance) would meet him
and proceed by team to our destination.

Having arranged all matters for our departure, on April 17, my wife,
her mother, our children and myself, took passage on a steamer to Terre
Haute; having shipped our household goods to St. Louis. We stayed overnight in Terre Haute, and from there went by rail to Champaign, Ill., in
the vicinity of which we spent several days visiting with friends. Leaving
there, we went via Springfield to St. Louis, stopping for a day and a night;
and from there by rail to Jefferson City, at that time the western termi-
nus of the only railroad in the state. We arrived there on the 27, or 28, of
April, as agreed upon with my brother, and found him waiting for us.

The information he brought was very encouraging as to the country, but he did not like the appearance of such of the company as he had seen, nor of the arrangements made on the company's location for the comfort of its members. He had met our Sec. Mr. Clubb, and found that he was a man of no experience of Western life and a new country and was, in his opinion, unfitted to manage the affairs of the company.

We had paid, I think, two ten cent assessments on our stock, and another due; but I have forgotten what amount of stock we then had. We concluded to withhold further payments until our arrival on the ground and decided as to our future action, after an examination of the conditions as we might find them.

Anxious to hasten on our journey, we set out on the same afternoon, on our way to our Kansas home. Hitherto we had traveled by steamer on the river, and by railroad, with all the comforts attending such travel. The Spring season was on, all nature was smiling, wood and landscape were all in beautiful green, and we were starting out with joyous feelings. On each side of our road were well improved farms, with fine houses and surroundings; the day was bright and warm, and we hoped to get out into the country a short distance and find a good camping place, and stop there for the night.

But just a little before night, there suddenly came up a hard thunderstorm, the rain falling in torrents; but our wagon cover was good, and we did not get wet. On account of the rain, and as that was our first night out, we began to look for a place where we could get accommodations in some house, and take some more favorable time for our first camping. While it was yet raining, a gentleman on horseback caught up with us, and entered into conversation; and as we neared his residence, he very politely invited us to go into his house and await the slacking of the rain, which offer we very gladly accepted.

He had a beautiful home, nicely set about with shrubbery and flowering plants. He was a southerner, with some slaves. After a time, as it was nearing night and the rain had nearly ceased, we suggested a desire to remain overnight; stating the fact that we were not very well equipped for camping out. To this suggestion, he very politely informed us that he could not accommodate us, but that he thought the rain would soon slack up, and that, at a house a ways beyond, thought we could get in for the night.

So, the rain ceasing for a time, we resumed our journey, only to meet with like receptions, until darkness began to shut down upon us, and we were becoming quite discouraged, when we came to a rather indifferent looking house to which we had been sent by the man to whom we had last applied for entertainment and been refused.

We found the family were "renters", with scant room for their own large family; but on learning of our situation, they at once gave us a hearty welcome, with such accommodations as they could offer, saying that they were not prepared to properly care for us, but that they could not turn women and children out, on such a night as that.

We learned that they were not native Missourians, and we made the best of the opportunity thankfully; and, in the morning, it having cleared off, we went on our way.

For the future, we provided ourselves with provisions, and as a rule, when night came, went into camp. We had no tent, the wagon cover was very good and would shed rain quite well; we had plenty of bedding, and the wagon offered a lodging place for the women and children, Samuel and I sleeping under the wagon, on the ground.

For about a week, the weather was very unsettled, raining more or less nearly every day or night. I think on the second night, we camped just at the bottom of a hill, near a small creek, and where the ground was dry. During the night, there came a hard, flooding rainstorm, Samuel and I were lying under the wagon where the water soon came rushing down the hill, driving us out of our sleeping place; and for the balance of that night we were camped in front of the wagon, inside, but with no chance for sleep.

The heavy rains soon made some of the streams impassable; and sometimes we pushed through swollen streams that were unsafe, but we met with no serious mishaps. When we had been about a week on the road, we reached the vicinity of the Osage river at Pappinville; there was a bridge across the river at this point, but the river had overflowed the bottom land on the other side for about seven miles; and, finding that it would be impossible for us to proceed further, we were fortunate in getting into a house with a family by the name of Dewese, who gave us a room with the privilege of using their stove for cooking; and here we put in eight days while waiting for the fall of the water.

Mr. Dewese was a northern man, and had no slaves; he owned a very good farm.

We were now nearing the Kansas line; there were but few slaves in this part of Missouri, most of the people having come from the North.

Hitherto, we had passed through parts where there were numerous slaves, but we never sought conversation with them, and if, at any time, we had occasion to speak with them, we were careful, as to what was said.

In our conversation with the slave-holders, we were equally careful not to give offence; still we never represented ourselves as holding other than Anti-Slavery sentiments. This course on our part seemed judicious, for the reason that just then excitement ran very high, and by the Missourian, persons passing through the state from the North to Kansas, were not generally looked upon with favor.

We, however, never had reason to fear any trouble from an expression of our political opinions.

While waiting here, we bought three yokes of oxen, finding that they were cheaper here than in Kansas, and knowing that we would need them for breaking the prairie.

It was about the 15th of May when the water had fallen so that we could cross the river and again proceed on our way.

Our delay had put us about a week or ten days behind the time we had set for our arrival at our destination. When we crossed the river on the bridge we found ourselves on a "bottom" road, on much of which, the water was still from one to two feet deep, and all very bad, making our progress very slow; in places, the pulling was very hard and through the mud and water, so that we had to attach one yoke of oxen with the horses, in order to make any headway. As it was, we found ourselves still in the mud and water when darkness began to shut us in. The road was through timber, very muddy and crooked, and we began to fear that we would not get out that night. Looking forward, we could see the lights from a house just outside the timber, maybe half a mile distant. Samuel took out one of the horses, and rode out to see if we could secure houseroom for the night; finding we could, and as we were all tired and worn out and hungry, he arranged with the woman to have us some supper prepared against our arrival. On his return, we took the two horses, Samuel getting on one, and I on the other, each of us taking on a woman behind and a child before; and thus we made our way out of that veritable "slough of despond". We turned the oxen loose, and started them ahead of us, expecting them to go to the prairie and graze on the grass, and that we would find them there in the morning.

We had a regular backwoods supper, which we greatly relished and enjoyed a good night's sleep, feeling that our travel troubles were over.

On getting up in the morning, we found two yoke of the oxen on the prairie, but one yoke was nowhere to be seen. After a time we thought that we had found their tracks leading back on the way we had come, and following on that distance of six or seven miles, through that miserable road of mud and water, we came to the bridge, and there they were—quietly lying down, having an aversion to going upon a bridge, they had laid down on dry ground off the approach. By the time we got them back, and the wagon out upon dry ground it was late in the afternoon, and we concluded to remain another night where we were. Here the woman of the house was kind enough to entertain our women with all kinds of stories of snakes, skunks, and wild-cats; filling their minds with great fear as to their future in this wild country.

The next morning was clear and warm, the sun shone brightly, and we started again upon our journey with high hopes of reaching the Kansas border during that day; the road was still muddy, so that our progress was slow, but in the afternoon, we passed out of Missouri and into Kansas, and camped for the night upon a small creek two or three miles northeast of Ft. Scott. Here we remained for one day; Samuel going into town to secure necessary supplies.

We were now within about fifty miles of our destination, which we hoped to reach within a couple of days. Our next day's travel was over a beautiful country, with here and there a settler along the streams, but with but little in the way of a road other than an Indian trail.

That night, we camped on the head of Elm Creek, a little timber along the same, but no settler in sight. The night was beautiful, a clear, balmy Kansas Spring night, with light of a full moon.

After supper, my wife and I were walking a little distance from the camp, admiring the beauties of the scenery, when, not far away in the timber, we heard the sharp cry of a panther or a catamount. The cry is startling, and sounds much like a human cry. We sought the camp without any unnecessary delay, and some of the more timid were more or less nervous during the remainder of the night; but we heard nothing further of its cry.

The next day we followed the course of Elm Creek, there being no wagon road. About noon, we came to a new town called "Cofachiqui", located near the Neosho river, and about two miles south of where Iola was afterwards located. The place was occupied at that time mostly by a company of Col. Buford's men, from Georgia, who had few slaves; and coming with the avowed purpose of assisting to make Kansas a Slave state. The legislature had designated the place as the County seat of Allen County, and at that time the settlers of the village and the surrounding country were nearly all "pro-slavery" in sentiment.

We did not like the appearance of these people, but passed on down the Neosho river that evening, reaching a point just a little south of where Humboldt now is, and near a settler by name of Henry Bennett, where we camped for the night. Mr. Bennett was the only settler near there, and we passed only two or three during the day, outside of those in the village of Cofachiqui. Mr. Bennett had come from Tennessee and was a strong "Free-State" man.

We were now within five miles of our destination; and on the next day, May 20, we reached the "promised land". We were not so badly disappointed as some others of our company, from the fact that Samuel had informed us as to what we might expect.

As voicing the general feeling of the members of our company on the ground before our arrival, I give the following from Mrs. Colt's book "Went to Kansas". She and her family arrived in the settlement about a week before our coming. Speaking of their arrival, she says:

"We leave our wagons and make our way to a large camp fire. It is surrounded by men and women, cooking their supper, while others are busy close by, grinding their hominy in hand mills. Look about, and see the grounds all around the camp fire are covered with tents in which the families are staying. Not a house is to be seen. The ladies tell us they are sorry to see us come to this place; which plainly shows us that all is not right. Can any one imagine our disappointment, on learning from this and that member that no mills have been built; that the directors, after receiving our money to build mills, have not fulfilled the trust reposed in them, and that, in consequence, some families have already left the settlement. For a moment, let me contrast the two pictures; the one we had made provision for and had reason to believe would be presented to us,

with the one that meets our eyes. We expected that a sawmill would be in operation, a grist mill building, and a temporary boarding house erected to receive families as they come into the settlement, until their own houses could be built. As it is, we find the families, some living in tents of cloth, some of cloth and green bark just peeled from the trees, and some wholly of green bark, stuck upon the damp ground without floors or fires".

Only two stoves in the company. These intelligent, but too confiding families have come from the North, East, South and West, to make pleasant homes; and now are determined to turn right-about, and start again on a journey, some know not where. Others have invested their all in the company; now come lost means and blighted hopes.

Sufficient to say, that we found conditions in no manner improved; one log house 16 x 16 feet, without floor, had been built, and was called the "Center House". It was located on the east side of the creek, named "Vegetarian Creek". In this, the Colt family was living; Mr. Clubb occupied an old Indian wigwam, covered with tenting cloth, south of the Center House. A family named Adams, lived in a log and bark shack a little north; the Broadbents were living in a cloth shack southwest, near the river; and a Mr. Herriman and the family were in a similar shack near Mr. Clubb. He and wife, with one child, had come from St. Louis in the wagon with Samuel, and while on the road, Mrs. Herriman gave birth to a child, only detaining them two days.

Others of the company were in a large tent, pitched on the high ground northeast of the old ford of the river. We availed ourselves, for the time being, of the shelter of this tent, in connection with the wagon cover.

One great difficulty with most of the members of the Company was their inability to adapt themselves to conditions unavoidable in frontier life; their expectations were too great as to the comforts and conveniences to be found under such conditions. They were mostly from the far East; mechanics, professional men, and men from offices and stores in the cities, and altogether unable to adjust themselves to a frontier life.

After spending one day in conversation with Mr. Clubb, our Secretary, and other members of the Company on the ground, we became convinced that the company would prove a failure.

We looked over the surrounding country for a few days, and were well pleased with the general appearance of the land, and resolved to remain. We bought a claimant out, who had selected a location just outside "Vegetarian Settlement", on the northwest, for which we paid him about $100.00 in a yoke of oxen.

The site for the building, in a beautiful grove, on high ground, we thought the most beautiful of any in all the country. But I will again quote from Mrs. Colt's book, "Went to Kansas".

"the Stewarts have located their claim west from here; and are building their cabin on a high prairie swell, where nature has planted the walnut and oak just sparsely enough for both beauty and shade. Just back, and south of the cabin is a ledge of shelving rocks where many berry bushes have taken root in the vegetable mould in their crevices, and are clinging for support to their craggy sides, grapevines clamber over rock, shrub and tree. There is a natural cut through the ledge, and an Indian trail leading down to a quiet little lake, sleeping among the tall grass, whose waters abound in fish and clams. The whole view is beautifully picturesque."

This site, we named "Cottage Grove", which name has been retained ever since. The Township in which it is situated, also bears the same name.

In reaching this period of my life, it now looks to me, after my life work. Hitherto, I had led a fairly comfortable, even course in life; had, for a number of years been engaged in a business congenial and fairly profitable; was happy in my family life, with wife and two children, all of whom had always lived in a city, surrounded with friends and most of the comforts of life. Here, we were on the frontier of civilization—indeed, just over the borderland; far away from a post-office, and over 100 miles from any town of importance—the nearest being Kansas City; with neither church nor school, and surrounded by strange, and for the most part, an uncongenial company of uncongenial spirits, united in a common effort to secure freedom for Kansas, and build up a strong colony of intelligent, temperate, liberal minded, right-living people, who would at once, by their combined efforts, secure schools, churches, mills, post office, and all the slow process usual in the settling of a new country.

But we found a majority of the company entirely unfitted to cooperate in securing the desired results; too many came without means, expecting to get employment from the company; those who had some means were so disposed to withdraw from the company; not willing to entrust their money with persons whom they found to be impracticable in methods of business. Of the officers, only the Secretary, Mr. Clubb, was on the ground; he had brought a small supply of groceries, for the use of the company; such as sugar, rice, beans, crackers, dried and canned fruits.

Some of the people thought that he had misappropriated the funds entrusted to him. I did not have that opinion of him, but I believed that he did not have the practical ability to manage the affairs of the company successfully. He was wholly unacquainted with Western life; he was an Englishman, about thirty years of age, with a wife but no children; had been connected with the New York Tribune, I think, as a reporter, and knew nothing outside of office work.

We therefore concluded to put nothing more into the company, but as we had "cut loose" from our Eastern relations, and "burned the bridges" behind us, we would remain in the country; having literally followed the advice of Horace Greeley, so often read, and "Go West" we would now try to "Grow up with the country."

It was now late in May, and our first thought was to break up some prairie, and get some things planted; corn, pumpkins, squashes, and melons, as well as some garden, for which we had brought an abundant supply of seeds. And here was a new experience for me, the driving of oxen. Samuel was, however, an expert at that; having worked with oxen when breaking prairie in Illinois. We broke out a few acres north and east of the building site, where we planted a variety of things; and in the meanwhile we went to work building the cabin of round rough logs, 16 x 18 feet square. This we built up to the square only, at the time, and added a shed on one side 8 or 10 feet wide for a kitchen; for a roof, we bought a large tent that had been used by the members of the company, who by this time had either gone to their own claims or had left the country; and this we drew over the top of our building, until such time as we could complete the roof.

On the sixth of June, we removed our effects to this place, as our future Home. We experienced much trouble in getting the logs for this cabin from the timber; the river had overflowed all the bottomland, and now in the timber the mosquitoes fairly swarmed. The weather was becoming hot, and while at work in the timber, we were compelled to wear our coats and tie handkerchiefs around our necks and over our faces, to as far as possible escape the torture of these pests.

A young man, by name of Buxton, who had come through with Samuel from St. Louis, had, since we selected our claim, been at work for us, made his home with us. Before moving into our cabin, we had sent him with the wagon and team of horses to Kansas City to get a lot of our goods which we had shipped to that point; and it was expected that it would take him about three weeks to make the trip.

I should have said, as to our house, that it had no floor; neither had we any table or bedsteads. We arranged our beds on one side of the house. About two feet from the ground, with a large auger, we bored holes in one of the logs, got poles about four feet long, sharpened one end, which we drove into the holes, letting the other end rest upon a stake driven into the ground; and up these, we built, with poles, brush, and grass, a bottom on which we placed our mattresses and bedding, forming a line of beds the entire length of the house.

We used boxes in which we had brought our goods, for a table, and for chairs, we resorted to various devices. We, however, had two or three chairs for the use of the women. We had brought with us a cook stove.

On the first night in our new home, there came up a flooding rain, with heavy thunder and lightning and a strong wind. For a time, the storm threatened to dismantle our abode by carrying away our tent covering; and Samuel and I were compelled to get up and hold on to it, to prevent its blowing away. As the sides of the house were quite open, the rain blew into it, and quite thoroughly wet everything within.

It was an unpleasant experience, for our first night, but the morning came bright and clear, as is its wont in "Sunny Kansas" and we felt reconciled to our condition.

Of the company, probably eight or ten families and several young men remained, and were engaged in putting in some crops, and improving the places which they still hoped to make homes for themselves; yet, for the most part, in a half-hearted way. It was very trying on the women of the party, most of whom had been accustomed to city life, or good society, in an old settled community of the East.

Here, settlers were few, and outside of our own company, were an uneducated, coarse class, mostly from Missouri and Arkansas, with more Indians than Whites as visitors; also, just at this time, in the North part of the Territory, there was much trouble between the settlers from the North and the "Border-Ruffians" from Missouri. We were not as yet troubled, but it was uncertain as to when the conflict might extend to us. The "Pro-Slavery" element was quite strong in our vicinity, and probably was, at that time, in the majority in the county.

Our nearest post-office was Ft. Scott, a distance of fifty miles; and to us who had been accustomed to a daily mail, it was a great deprivation. We soon arranged to have someone go once a week for the mail. Samuel often went for it, taking three days to make the round trip. It was a great event, each Saturday night, to get dozens of letters and papers by one mail, and we would sit up nearly all the night to read over letters from friends far away, as, also the papers which were very full of accounts of the troubles in "Bleeding Kansas."

We began to feel some concern about Mr. Buxton and our household goods, after he had been gone about three weeks, with no word from him. We could hear many reports of trouble about Lawrence, and of Northern men being turned back on their way through Missouri to Kansas, and of raids from the vicinity of Kansas City and Westport. We began to fear that we would never see more of Buxton, Team, or goods; when, one day we saw Buxton coming over the prairie, afoot and alone. Indeed, he was as disconsolate a looking person as one could imagine. He was an Englishman, of slender build, with serious countenance, ordinarily; but on that occasion, his face was unusually elongated, and expression most forlorn.

His story was soon told. He had secured the goods, consisting of a large hogshead packed with chinaware, with articles of clothing and bedding among it, a bookcase, packed with books and bedding; and some other things in boxes. He had also some groceries and a prairie breaking-plow that he had bought for us all in the wagon.

He had looked around and loaded up in Kansas City, and started home. It should be stated, that at that time, Kansas City consisted of a few warehouses on the front of the river, and a few businesses and residences on the bluffs, it was, indeed, called "Westport Landing," Westport being the main town, four miles out on the state line.

He had reached Westport, when a party of armed men stopped him on the principal street, and informed him that they wanted his horses; took off the harness, putting it into the wagon, which they pulled into an alley; they told Mr. Buxton that he could go his way. He could do nothing else than make his way on foot. It took him about ten or twelve days to return; much of the way without roads other than Indian trails, and the country being but sparsely settled, so that sometimes he had difficulty in getting either food or shelter.

We realized that we had, indeed, fallen upon troublous times. Our loss would be at least $500.00, and one not easily borne by us in our circumstances. In the hope that some part of our property might be recovered, Samuel took a pony we had brought with us from Indiana and started to Kansas City. On arriving there he found the wagon where it had been left, with harness and boxes of goods intact. The box containing the bookcase had been opened, but finding books and not "Sharps Rifles" as they no doubt suspected, nothing was taken.

The groceries and prairie plow were taken. Samuel, with the friendly aid of a Mr. McGee, a pro-slavery man, secured one of the horses, it having been left in a stable on account of having become lame; both horses had been used by the "Missouri Raiders" in making a foray into the territory; the one was still out in the service. He got possession of the one horse, but not being able to get the other, he hitched up the pony with the horse recovered, and came home.

His home-coming was a matter of much rejoicing, for while our fine team was broken, we felt thankful that we had come out so well.

We never saw more of the lost horse. In the meantime, summer was upon us. The season was favorable to the growth of our garden stuff and other crops, and we began to have a few green things to eat. We found fine blackberries along the edge of the timber, and especially an abundance of very fine ones along Big Creek, some eight miles south of our place. We had also bought a very good cow, and had plenty of milk and butter. The river, in the spring, had flooded the lowlands, and now malaria began to affect many of our neighbors; mosquitoes were also very troublesome, so very persistent were they, that it became impossible to sleep in our cabin, too open to keep them out, and, as a rule, we were compelled to take out a couple of blankets and sleep on the ground on the open prairie, where the breeze would, in a measure, drive them away.

The dews were very heavy and this may have contributed to the attacks of chills and fever. Whatever the cause, many of our people became ill, and our numbers were decreased by still further desertions.

By the middle of the summer, we had put a roof on our cabin, chinked and daubed up the sides, and had secured some hewed-out boards, which the company had made to be used in the works of a contemplated mill; these, we used to make a very substantial door; and for a floor overhead, we had gone to an old deserted Indian village, and got a lot of "Puncheons", made by the squaws and used by them in the construction of their wigwams. These boards were about five feet long and from eighteen inches to four feet wide, dressed down to from one to two inches in thickness. It was a wonder how they could have dressed them out of large trees, in some cases as much as four feet in diameter.

In the building of a wigwam, they first took long poles, setting one end into the ground, in two parallel rows, about 12 or 15 feet apart, for a distance of 20 to 50 feet, bending the tops over so as to meet, forming an oval top, then they placed these boards, or "puncheons" on end along the sides and ends, leaving an opening at one end for ingress and egress; then, from the tops of these boards, over the top of the wigwam, would be covered with a matting of skins, leaving an opening in the center for the smoke to pass out. A fire was built on the ground in the center of the wigwam, where the cooking was done, and around which the family sat by day and slept at night.

In a village, the wigwams were arranged in lines, fronting a street, often as many as thirty or forty. We found one of these deserted villages, seven miles down the river, with wagon loads of these puncheons on the ground. It was a wonder to us, why they should have left such quantities of boards, the making of which must have taken so much time and labor. The settlers hauled them away, using them in various ways, about their places.

We noticed that when the Indians saw these boards, they were talking together about our use of them, and we inferred that they were displeased that we had appropriated them as we had. Imagine our feelings, when later, we learned that a few years before, this village had been scourged with an epidemic of small-pox! Which had abandoned the place. Fortunately, any germs of the disease left behind had perished before we became possessed of the boards.

After we had got floors in our cabin, below and above, we were the most comfortably fixed of all the families in the settlement; so that when sickness became general among the members of our company on occasion, our house became a sort of hospital for the sick who could not as well be cared for at their own homes; we sometimes had the house quite full of such cases.

We, having come from a malarious country, did not so readily succumb to the disease here. My wife and her mother seemed immune, as also did Samuel; the children and myself were, in the end, more or less victims of the disease. Mr. Buxton had quite a siege of the chills and fever.

We also had, for some time with us, sick Mr. Wheeler, a young man, and Mrs. Barker, a widow from New York City, and others. None of these persons were very ill, and all, during the summer, left the country.

In the meantime we were cultivating our little crop, and making such improvements as we could, on our claim. Yet we were not greatly encouraged, the unsettled condition of affairs in the territory prevented immigration; there was much sickness among our people; and quite general discouragement, so that many were leaving, while none were coming to take their places. Our number was decreasing, rather than increasing. We also learned that we might have trouble as to our lands. It was unsurveyed, we knew, when making the settlement; but now it was understood that we were on Indian lands, from which we were liable to be removed at any time.

Our secretary, Mr. Clubb, took down with the chills and fever; and as he saw the members of his company leaving, one by one, while those remaining were only awaiting an opportunity to leave, he also became discouraged; and Samuel started with him and his wife to Kansas City about the middle of August; at Kansas City they found the people were not permitted to pass into the Territory. Samuel found that he could not return without trouble, and he sought the aid of his former friend, McGee; but the feeling was so intense that he could not get permission to come. After waiting two or three days, with no better success, he adopted a plan by which he got out of the City. He took down the bows and cover of the wagon, bought a broad-brimmed straw hat, and having oxen hitched to his wagon, he assumed the role of a countryman, started out into Missouri, and thus got out of the City into the country; and after going a few miles, he turned in a southern course, through the state, until near Ft. Scott, when he succeeded in crossing the line into Kansas. However, he had much trouble in passing through Missouri, having been stopped on two or three occasions.

In the early part of September, the family of Colt's left the settlement, W. H. Colt, wife and two children; one of our best families. They were from New York, were well educated and highly refined.

Mr. Colt and both children had been, for several weeks, sick with the chills and fever. Mr. Colt's father, mother and sister remained.

The family started in a wagon for some railroad point in Missouri, with a view of taking passage for their former home; on reaching Boonville, Mr. Colt became too ill to travel further. And here, both he and the boy died; the widow and daughter proceeding on their way until friends were reached in Michigan.

Thus, one after another of our company left us; very few of those remaining had any intention of making permanent homes in Kansas. They waited only for opportunities to get away. Two brothers, Broadbents, from Tennessee, stalwart Scotchmen, in full vigor of manhood, were living alone in a tent, about a mile east of our place, and were for some time ailing, but I had no thought that they were dangerously sick; when, through a neighbor, I learned that one of them was dead and the other very low; both were dead within two days.

While many had been sick with chills and fever, no one of our company had, hitherto, died. They had died without medical attention, and with but scant help from anyone. A nearby neighbor had called on them daily, and had given them fresh water, and such help as seemed called for, but, as for a doctor, there was none within fifty miles.

And now, as to their burial; there was no undertaker, and no lumber with which to make a coffin, nearer than Ft. Scott, fifty miles; what should we do? We selected as fair boards of the Indian puncheons mentioned before, as we could, and formed very rude boxes from them, into which we placed the bodies, burying them on a slope of the prairie, a little distance from the tent in which they had died.

Samuel and I, with another neighbor, dug the graves just over a swell of prairie, and out of sight of our cabin, that the women there might not see, and thus learn that death had come so near to us.

Some little time after, we were called upon to perform a like service for a young man named Curtis, who had come from Connecticut; and refused to leave with his son, a few weeks before. Of this event, Mrs. Colt in her book "Went to Kansas" says:

"Kind neighbors came in and dressed the cold form of the departed for the grave. They nailed together some of the rough "puncheons" which they had taken from the wigwam ruins, for a coffin, wrapped him in winding sheet and Indian blanket, and laid him therein; then bore him away without prayer, requiem or knell, and laid him in his

narrow home beneath the rich soil of the prairie, on whose bosom were still blossoming many a richly tinted flower."

Thus, four of our members were dead, and nearly all the living ones had left us. One of these four in question was old Mr. Colt, to whom the foregoing excerpt refers. The situation was anything but encouraging. The unsettled condition, generally over the Territory, was not improving; large bodies of Pro-slavery men from Missouri and Arkansas were invading the Territory; "Free-state" parties from the East were stopped in Missouri at different points, and turned back. Many free-state settlers in our part of the Territory were becoming discouraged and leaving; while settlers from the South, not being so liable to malarial troubles, and inured to the privations and hardships of frontier life, were remaining.

As to our success in raising crops, we could not, in the nature of things, expect much; and I and all being new, had nothing planted before June. We raised some garden stuff, plenty of pumpkins, squashes, and melons, but very little corn. I had learned to handle oxen, so that I could yoke up and drive them fairly well.

While we cultivated friendship with the Indians, and were not fearful of any violence on their part, we were constantly subject to their thieving propensities, they would steal green corn, potatoes, or melons, under our very eyes; and I never thought of leaving the family alone, either by day or by night. We, however, gained the friendship of some of the leading members of the tribe, which, I think, stood in good stead, on occasion. We often had them with us at dinner, or other meals, and many times some of them would remain with us overnight, in which case, if the night was cold, they would lie down on the floor in front of the fire, sometimes as many as half a dozen at a time.

As the winter approached, we built a stone fire-place and chimney, and, as I was a stonecutter, we made us a neatly cut stone fireplace, with dressed stone chimney throughout.

Our cabin was a very rough log building, but when finished up for the winter it was very comfortable; and was superior to any other house in that country, at the time. The cold of winter seemed to have destroyed the fever germs, we all regained a good degree of health, and thus were in better spirits.

During the winter, we got out much fencing material. I was no hand to either chop the timber, or to make rails, but I could drive the oxen, and haul the rails out of the timber. We hired two men from the north part of the county to come and make several thousand rails and posts. These were all hauled onto our claim, where we intended making fences in the spring; all in readiness for making extensive improvements in the way of farming more land.

In the Territory, 1857 opened up under more favorable conditions for the "Free-state men of the Territory." The laws passed by the Legislature of 1855, commonly called the "bogus laws" had been wholly ignored by the Free-state men of the territory. The Topeka Constitution had been adopted by the freestate voters; and, under it, a Legislature had been elected. Our part of the Territory had enjoyed quiet during the winter; we had some Free-state families come into the neighborhood in the spring; among them, my uncle, F. W. Stewart and family; also the family of Dr. I. N. Phillips, from Illinois, and a number of German families.

However, the Topeka Constitution, and the legislature under it were not recognized by the General Government, and on its meeting in Topeka in January, the presiding officers of both houses were arrested with several of the members, and taken to Tecumseh, before Judge Cato, and bound over to the U. S. Court, the legislature being without a quorum, took a recess till June. The second session of the Territorial Legislature met in Lecompton, in January, John W. Geary being the Governor; he and the legislature did not agree, and later he resigned.

The Free-state men had, hitherto, refrained from voting, but during the summer, a feeling grew that by taking part in the elections they could elect a "Free-state" Legislature, and get control of the Territorial government; and later, when, in September, Governor Walker issued an address assuring the people that in October, election should be fairly conducted, the Free-state men were disposed to take him at his word; a Free-state convention having been held at Grasshopper Falls, of which my brother was a member; resolved to take part in the Fall elections.

As a result of that election, Samuel became a member of the House of Representatives. He was also elected a member of the Legislature under the Topeka Constitution.

Early that spring, a post office was established at Cofachiqui, but no mail service was put on, and the settlers arranged with someone to carry the mail from Ft. Scott, weekly, as had been done before.

A son was born on April 8th, we named him Fred. The following letter written to our afflicted friend Mrs. Colt, will fairly express my feelings, at this time:

Neosho, Kansas, May 17, 1857

Dear Mrs. Colt:

Yours of March 30 was but recently received. We had thought and spoken of you, very often, and in every mail had hoped to hear from you, but did not, until a short time before receiving your letter, hear of your great bereavement. Mr. Moorhees then wrote us of it.

Be assured, Mrs. Colt, you have, our tenderest sympathies, in this, your great affliction, bitter indeed, has been your cup. What a destruction of family, in one short year! How soon our fondest hopes may all be crushed, crushed.

To us, the past year has been one of many hardships and troubles, but our lives have been spared; and since about the time you left, we have enjoyed good health. We have got things fixed up around, so that we now live quite comfortably.

Samuel, our brother who went to take Clubb to Kansas City, got home the evening after you left, in good health.

He had some narrow escapes, and to get home was obliged to go round through Missouri 100 miles out of his way.

Mr. Adams went, shortly after you left, to Maysville, Arkansas. We had a letter from them in the winter, their health had improved. The Broadbents both died, shortly after, old Mr. Colt.

Mr. Hobbs went back to Ohio. Mrs. Barker remained with us until late in the Fall, then went to Kansas City, with the intention of going home. Buxton is still in the neighborhood; Blackburn went to Tennessee, home to his family.

Immigration is coming in very fast, and we are getting many new neighbors. There is a town laid off, up the river five miles, and a steam mill is to be put up there, this summer. Altogether, the prospects for us in the future, are encouraging.

Mrs. Stewart has a son, born April 8th. She is very well.

We would be gratified to have you write soon again. Receive our best wishes for your future.

Respectfully,
Watson and Elizabeth

CHAPTER 5

OF LARCENY AND THE LEGISLATURE

The town of "Humboldt" was laid out that spring, by a company from Lawrence, composed largely of Germans. The first house built was one of logs, for J. A. Coffey, by my uncle, F. W. Stewart. It was built on contract, for $25.00. Early in the summer, a steam sawmill was put up by Orlin Thurston. It was considered a great acquisition, as there was no other mill within 50 miles. We felt greatly encouraged to see a town starting up within five miles of us, where we could purchase some of the necessaries, and could get lumber.

We extended our cultivated land by breaking out and fencing in quite a large field east of our house, putting it into sod-corn, melons and pumpkins. Others, of our relatives, came out from Illinois during that summer, Uncle Daniel Stewart and family, cousins David Stewart with family and his brother, John. These additions to our immediate neighborhood were very gratifying.

At the fall election the Free-state party elected a large majority of the members of both branches of the Territorial Legislature, and in our own county, the Free-state party obtained complete control. I think it was at the election in the spring of 1858 that I was elected one of the Justices of the Peace, for Allen County, and it so happened that I was the only one to qualify. The result was that all business of that kind in the county came before me, and I was kept quite busy; some rather important cases coming before me.

We had cherished the thought of sometime building us a residence with concrete walls; and to test the practicability of the matter, we built a small house in this way, about ten by sixteen feet, one story, with cellar. We built a large log-heap in the timber, on which we piled limestone and then fired the logs, which, in burning, reduced the stone to lime; and thus we secured the lime for the walls. The lime, we mixed with sand and rough stone, and this mixture we put into boxes formed by boards about a foot wide, set apart the width of the thickness of the wall; and we had a very useful building, which we used for various purposes, one of which was as an office for holding my court. And, later, we laid in a small stock of such goods as were desired by the Indians, and opened up quite a profitable trade with them.

They had mostly, for trade, Buffalo robes and ponies. We could get the robes for about $4.00 each, and ponies at from $10.00 to $20.00 each. We gave them flour, sugar, coffee and tobacco; also, goods for the Squaw's dresses, and blankets.

As there was considerable immigration to our part of the Territory, this year, there was much trouble as to claims. The settlers had formed a sort of Protective League, in which was recognized the right of each settler to hold a claim, independent of the one on which he resided. All of which had no support under the U. S. laws; but the settlers set up a "higher law", and, for a time, enforced it. Speculation in claims became quite a business; persons leaving the country would sell their claims for such price as they could get, and the purchaser would hold and sell to the newcomer for, sometimes, two or three times the amount paid.

This practice was finally broken up, when one A. W. J. Brown, living in the north part of the county, sold one such claim to a Mr. Rhodes for about $2,000.00, receiving, I think, $600.00 in cash and taking a note for the balance. This note, when due, Rhodes refused to pay, and suit was brought in the U. S. Court for its collection, where the action, of course, failed.

As to the claim of a prairie and timber tract of 320 acres, it having no warrant in law, as settlers came in and began to contest such claims, they were abandoned, each settler being restricted to 160 acres.

While in our part of the Territory, we were enjoying peace and quiet, there was much political agitation over the rest of the Territory. The Lecompton Constitution had been formed without being submitted to the people for adoption or rejection. The Territorial Legislature had ordered an election for a vote on the Constitution, at which time it was almost unanimously rejected, the Pro-Slavery party generally not voting; this vote was on January 4.

The same month, the Legislature under the Topeka Constitution met, but did little business.

In the meantime, a Constitutional Convention, of which my brother was a delegate, met in March, at Maneola, and adjourned to Leavenworth, where a Constitution was formed, known as the "Leavenworth Constitution."

There was much disturbance along the Kansas border, in Lynn and Bourbon Counties. At one point in Lynn county, a band of men from Missouri crossed the line and arrested nine "Free-state" men, and taking them near the Missouri line, stood them in line and fired on them— when everyone fell, all shot to death or wounded. One of the wounded men was afterwards shot dead; six were killed, the other three feigned death, and thus escaped. One, Asa Hairgrove, I became acquainted with in Montgomery County, many years afterwards.

These disturbances did not extend to our section of the Territory, in fact, the settlers in Allen County, of all parties, agreed in Convention, that we would resist any invasion of our county by any armed force, of whatever party.

In the Fall of this year, the post office was established at Humboldt, and a weekly service from Lawrence was put on. Albert Irwin was the first Postmaster; and thus we had a post-office within five miles, and regular mail once a week. In the meantime, Humboldt had become quite a village. W. C. O'Brien had put up a steam saw-and-grist mill.

The year of 1858 was not noted, in our part of the Territory, for any unusual occurrence; and County received a large acquisition of Northern Settlers, and many of the Pro-slavery settlers sold their claims and left the country; so that the county had a good majority of Free-state men, and the government of the county was in their hands; and, as to the Territory, there was no longer any doubt as to the Free-state element controlling it, and in the end, establishing a state government under a constitution excluding slavery.

There was still more or less trouble along the eastern border, in Lynn and Bourbon Counties. Gangs from Missouri made occasional raids over the line, attempting to drive out Free-state settlers, killing them and burning their houses; and the settlers on this side, under such men as John Brown and James Montgomery, organized for their own protection; and, no doubt, excesses were committed on both sides. During the season, we had broken out a tract in the bottom west of the lake in addition to the land cultivated east of the house on the high prairie. Our thought, on first settlement, was that the bottom land would not be desirable for cultivation, on account of its liability to overflow; but we learned from the Indians and others that the river did not flood these lands only once in several years.

We therefore changed our claim lines, so as to include the bottom land lying west and south of the lake; and we soon learned from the better crops yielded by these bottom lands, that we had chosen wisely.

We had accrued a few fruit trees and set them out on the slope north of the house, but were anxious for more of an orchard, and I took a lot of the Buffalo robes that we had obtained from the Indians, and went over into Southwest Missouri, to the Counties of Cedar and Polk, and traded them for apple trees, and winter apples, and some other articles of use to us, and in the spring of 1859, we set out quite an orchard.

For us, the year of 1859 was a fairly prosperous one, as to crops; and the general condition of the country was encouraging.

In May, a Convention was held at Osawatomie by the Free-state party, which was addressed by Horace Greeley. The Convention adopted a platform, and organized as the Republican Party. Hitherto, all those persons who favored the admission of Kansas as a "Free" state, had united and acted together under the name of the "Free-State" party.

In June, delegates were elected to form another Constitution. These delegates met in Wyandotte July 5th, and formed the Constitution, which, on October 4th, was adopted by a large majority of the voters; and under this Constitution, the State was finally admitted.

Early in this year, our neighborhood was very much annoyed by a system of thievery that had grown up among quite a number of settlers.

The Indians would occasionally steal horses from the settlers, and by way of reprisal, a number of rather rough characters, mainly from Missouri, united in the business of running off Indian ponies to Missouri, and selling them or trading them for horses or cattle, which they would bring back to the settlement.

The business had been carried on for several months, and the Indians were becoming very restless. There would be quite a herd of ponies missing, and at the same time some of the parties would also be gone, who, after a week or two, would return with the proceeds of their trip. Soon, these persons became well known to both Indians and the whites, as being engaged in this wholesale thievery. The Indians would miss a lot of ponies, and would go from house to house, and, finding that certain of these men were gone, would come to us with their complaints, seeming to think that we were leading men, and could, in some manner, help them to recover their ponies, or prevent our neighbors from stealing them. A few of the white settlers who were opposed to this business, finally arranged

with a few friendly Indians to go on a certain night and capture some of
the most notorious characters, and give them a good scare, indeed, such a
scare as would compel them to leave the country.

In accordance with this plan, on a certain night, the Indians went
from house to house, gathering in four or five of these men, they were
George Kelly, Ed Marble, and two Galloway brothers, and, I think, one
other person. These, they carried off a distance of seven or eight miles,
to Godfrey's trading post on Big Creek, where were two or three Indian
chiefs, and a number of other Indians. A council was held, after which
ropes were put around the men's necks, and they were made to understand that they were to be hung. Of course they were informed as to
the reason for such punishment. They promised to quit the business,
and begged for their lives, but the Indians gave them no hope; but, on
their earnest solicitation, the matter was held in abeyance until Dr.
Phillips and my brother could be sent for.

On their arrival, and after a full consultation between the Dr.,
Samuel, and the Indians, it was agreed to spare their lives upon the following conditions, viz.: The names of all persons connected with them
in the "Business" should be divulged, while each of the parties under arrest should submit to the shaving of one side of his head; that, at once
upon being released, they should give notice to each of the parties impli-
cated with them to leave the country within ten days; and that they would
do the same, promising never to return, under penalty of certain death if
found in the country after ten days.

These conditions being accepted by them, the parties were set free after the shaving of one side of their heads. I was not personally concerned
in these proceedings, but was in very hearty sympathy, and on the following day it did me much good to see some of these men going about the
neighborhood with shaved heads, making arrangements for a final leave
of the country; which they were careful to do within the agreed time.

The clearing out of these thieves was felt to be a great boon to the community in general; and the effect on the Indians was very beneficial in the establishing of a kindly feeling towards the whites remaining.

In the early autumn, at Ft. Scott, a Republican convention for the twelfth Council district, honored me with the nomination as Councilman in the Territorial Legislature. The district was composed of the counties of Bourbon, Allen, McGee, Dorn, Woodson, and Wilson. The Council was the upper house of the legislature, and consisted of thirteen members. I was not at the convention, and nomination was wholly without solicitation on our part. After a time, I learned that the Democratic party had placed in nomination one N. S. Goss, of Neosho Falls, Woodson county; a gentleman who had built a water-mill at that place, and of whom I had heard, but with whom I was not personally acquainted. I felt quite certain of my election, as I understood the district was safely Republican, although in and about Ft. Scott, the Democratic element was dominant. Some two weeks before the election, while engaged in the bottom field, across the lake, in digging potatoes, (of which we had a very fine crop) Mr. Goss called upon me. He said that he had come down to Humboldt and, learning where I lived, had thought it well to call upon me and become acquainted. It was nearly noon, and I invited him to go to the house and have dinner, which invitation he accepted.

I took him to the cabin, introduced him to my wife, and we were soon enjoying a good dinner together. I found him to be a very pleasant gentleman; he suggested that we make a canvass of the district together; I told him that I had not sought the nomination; that I was not a political speaker, and had not intended to leave my home to make a canvass, but would rely upon my friends to say, by their votes, whether or not they wanted me to represent them. He finally concluded to adopt my policy, and returned home, expressing his belief that I would be elected, and the hope that his interests would be well guarded by me, in certain local legislation; and, from that meeting, on for many years, in my intercourse with Mr. Goss, I found him a gentleman in the fullest sense of the word.

The entire vote in the district was 1192, of which I received 642, thereby winning the election by 92 votes.

Lincoln visited Kansas in December, making speeches in Leavenworth and Atchison.

My son Joseph was born October 30. He came into the world without the aid of either doctor or midwife. We had expected to have Dr. Phillips living within two miles of us, but it chanced that he was away from home. I went about a mile to get my aunt Catherine Stewart, leaving my wife alone with her mother, and on my return found that the boy had been born. We named him for my father, all turned out well, for both mother and child.

The Territorial Legislature met January 2, 1860. Some days earlier I had a chance to ride to Lawrence with Mr. Jordan Neal, who resided near that place, and who, with his wife, was visiting his cousin, Moses Neal, in Humboldt. There was a stage line, but I gladly accepted the chance to go with Mr. Neal, wife, and two children, in his carriage. I arrived in Lawrence January 21st, where the members of the Legislature were in waiting, with a view of driving up to Lecompton the next morning; Lecompton being the place designated for the meeting of the Legislature; but, because the place had been named as the Capital by the Pro-slavery party, and was not very well provided for the accommodation of the members, the meeting of the Legislature, the former Legislature had adjourned to, and held its session in Lawrence, and I found the people of Lawrence making every possible effort to secure similar action on our part.

The City offered a hall for the meetings, free of charge; and the hotels made very favorable rates to the members; and the Republican members were, generally, in favor of meeting at Lecompton the next day, and immediately adjourning to Lawrence.

I was stopping at the Eldridge house, the principal hotel, a very fine one, for the times. It was, in fact, a house built to replace the "Free-state

Hotel" which had been destroyed during the Missouri Invasion of 1856. During the evening, I met the notorious James H. Lane, a man of whom much had been said for and against; a man who had come to Kansas a Democrat, but who, on seeing the methods adopted by the Democratic party to fasten slavery upon the Territory, had espoused the "Free-state" cause, and was now a leader of the radical wing of the Republican party.

Unfortunately, in a claim difficulty, he had shot the contestant, Gaius Jenkins, and lost the respect of many of the party's friends, so much so, that the party had become divided into Lane and anti-Lane factions, and the feeling was becoming very bitter. Whatever the merits in the case may have been, I, at the time, had made up my mind that I would act with the anti-Lane party. However, I met the man; he found that I was from Indiana, his native state; he offered me a seat in his buggy on the next morning, and with him I rode to Lecompton, much of my prejudice having worn away in the meantime. I found that Lane had friends enough in the Legislature to organize it in his interest. The body was composed of thirteen members of the Council, and thirty-nine members of the House. We organized the Council by the election of W. W. Updegraff as President, and John J. Ingalls as Secretary. There were eight members returned as Republicans, and five as Democrats. The seat of one Democrat was contested, and the Republican member seated, thus giving nine Republicans and four Democrats.

On the second day of the session, we passed a joint resolution adjourning to meet in Lawrence on the seventh; Samuel Medary was Governor, and he promptly vetoed the resolution, which, was as promptly, passed over his veto, and hied away to Lawrence. The citizens of Lawrence furnished transportation for the members and Legislative supplies, records, etc, free of charge; halls for the meetings without cost, also very low rates for the members at the hotels. At that time, there was no railroad, and everything had to be transported by wagon. I was furnished a nice room, in connection with two other members, warmed and lighted, with board, at three dollars per week, at the Eldridge house, the best one in the place.

We were much better located, as to our own comfort and convenience in Lawrence than we could have been at Lecompton, but the action of the Legislature in the removal, was one of sentiment, rather than of necessity. Lecompton had been designated as the Capital of the Territory by the general government, at the behest of the Slavery interests; and the Free-state people had built up Lawrence. The Government had spent $50,000.00 toward the erection of a Capitol building, which had been spent in laying the foundation, and beginning the walls of the building which the Free-state party had determined should never be utilized for the purposes intended.

We met in Lawrence as per adjournment, but the Governor refused to recognize us, remaining, himself, at Lecompton.

We continued our sessions until the 18th, when we adjourned. It was, however, understood that the Governor would immediately call us together again, in extra session, at Lecompton, this he did. We met on the 19th, and at once adjourned to meet in Lawrence on the 21st. The Governor went with us; and the work of the session began.

We did not enact many laws of general interest; the Wyandotte Constitution had been voted on and adopted at the Fall election, and State officers and members of the legislature were elected; and we were only awaiting the action of Congress, to become a sovereign State.

A large number of local bills were passed, such as the incorporation of Town Companies, etc. At that time, also, there was a great demand for legislative action in the dissolving of the marriage relation, and many divorces were granted; which action, I with a few other members, in every case opposed. We found that Slavery existed under the laws of the Territory, and passed a bill abolishing it. Every Republican in both houses voted for it, and every Democrat voted against it. The Governor vetoed the bill, and we passed it over the veto. Mr. Beeve, a Democrat of the Council, in a minority report from the Committee, said, "We have found that there is now invested in this Territory, between one fourth and one half million of dollars worth of property in slaves, and, believing that the immediate prohibition of an existing right of property in any given article, is beyond either the Legislative power of the States or Territories; as contravening the letter and the spirit of Articles Four and Five of the amendments to the Federal Constitution; recommend to your honorable body the indefinite postponement of the said bill."

The Democratic Territorial Convention met at Atchison in March, and also denounced the action of the Legislature in passing this bill for the abolishing of Slavery.

We adjourned on the 27th of February.

My recollections of this winter, spent as a legislator, are very pleasant; our body of only thirteen members seemed like an orderly debating club; some of the members were quite able, in debate; four were Democrats, and nine, Republicans. The minority had a decided advantage, as to ability in debate. W. C. Mathias, of Leavenworth, was a Democrat, and a lawyer; he had been a member of the first Territorial Legislature, in 1855; commonly known as the "bogus legislature." George M. Beebe was a Democrat from Doniphan, also a lawyer of good speaking ability; he was afterwards appointed Territorial Secretary, and during the absence of the Governor, for a short time, he was the acting Governor; and he was so acting at the time of the admission of Kansas as a state.

He removed to New York, and was a member of Congress for one term, at least, there.

On the Republican side, our best debaters were W. W. Updegraff and P. P. Elder. Mr. Elder, in 1861, was appointed Osage Indian Agent; in 1870, he was elected Lieutenant Governor; and later, he went off with the Populist movement, and was, for several years, prominent in their councils; he still lives, at a ripe old age, in Ottawa. Our Secretary, John J.

Ingalls, was a bright young lawyer, of Sumner, Atchison county, a young man of fine ability; was a member of the State Senate in 1862; filled many places of trust, in after years, and was in the U. S. Senate for eighteen years, succeeding S. C. Pomeroy in 1873. In the U. S. Senate, he was recognized as one of its most brilliant members, in debate.

1860 was noted as the year of the great drought, in Kansas. There was a very general failure of crops, over the entire Territory; while in the southern part, the failure was complete. The previous fall and winter were very dry, and during the spring and summer, but very little rain fell; the summer was very hot, and vegetation and crops planted, having moisture enough to bring them through the ground, withered and died; our lake dried up; on our farm, we did not raise a bushel of corn, and but little garden stuff. We had got a start in stock, but what hogs we had, we sold to a party who drove them to Missouri where feed could be had, we got $1.25 per 100 lbs. For our cattle, we depended upon the timber grass for their winter feed.

Many of the settlers having friends in the East, received aid from them; others left the country; many were unable to leave, and, without aid from abroad, must suffer. Our part of the Territory, being newlaid, had but little left over from last year's crop, upon which to subsist; consequently, all of our supplies must be hauled in from Kansas City of Southwest Missouri. My brother, in the fall, in behalf of the settlers of Allen County, made a trip to Illinois, Indiana and Ohio, where he was acquainted, soliciting and receiving, for our aid, a very liberal donation. Thadeus Hyatt, of New York, with W. R. M. Arney, and S. C. Pomeroy of Kansas, visited the county to ascertain the condition of the people, and, at a meeting at Humboldt, they informed the settlers that provisions, clothing, etc., would be sent from the East, to be distributed to those in need, through Mr. Pomeroy at Atchison; and I was designated as an Agent for Cottage Grove township, to receive and distribute such aid; and, in furtherance of that plan, I went to Atchison with a number of settlers with teams to procure such aid as our township was entitled to receive. I think we had about twenty teams, and we made the trip in December, taking, I think, seventeen days to do it. We had rather cold disagreeable weather; some snow; and we camped out every night. On reaching Atchison, we found the demand was very great, while the supply was but scant; we, however, brought back such supplies as we could get, received thankfully. However, I think its entire value would not have been equal to a dollar a day for each person and team in the company, still, it helped us out, and we were very glad to get it, indeed, but for the help sent us from the East, there would have been much suffering in Kansas.

Earlier in the fall, I had made two trips to Missouri and Arkansas, bringing out supplies of corn meal, flour, and apples, mostly the proceeds of the Buffalo robes which we had received in our trade with the Indians; and, in this way, we were able to get through that winter with a minimum of discomfort.

The year of 1861 came in with Kansas still a Territory; and on the seventh of January, the Legislature met at Lecompton and, as usual, adjourned to Lawrence, where its sessions were held until the bill admitting us as a state, was passed by Congress. The bill passed the Senate January 21, the House on the 28th, and was signed by the President on the 29th, and thus ended our struggle for Statehood.

The Legislature did but little business, and I returned home to resume my work on the farm. Charles Robinson was sworn in as Governor, February 9, and the first Legislature met March 26th, and on April 4, S. C. Pomeroy and J. H. Lane were elected U. S. Senators.

The spring opened up with promise of good crops, and we felt encouraged as to the future. The crop failure of the past year had discouraged many of the settlers; some having left the country, and conditions were not favorable to immigration. The survey of the New York Indian lands, on which we had supposed we were settled, had shown that we were on the Osage Indian lands, and these Indians looked upon us as trespassers.

The Government had, the Fall before, ordered the settlers off the Cherokee Neutral lands, lying in Crawford and Cherokee Counties; and on their failure to leave, a posse of soldiers had gone from house to house, giving settlers time to remove furniture and other belongings from the houses, had then set fire to their houses, thus leaving them out in inclement weather, without house or home. I thought, at the time, such action on the part of the Government was most atrocious; and I still think it an act without one redeeming feature in its justification; it was done in the interest of the Slave power. There was not then, nor never had been, any of these lands on which these people were settled, any Indians; and no Indian was benefited by the dispossessing of these settlers of their homes and crops; and these settlers had raised more crops, that year of drouth, than any other part of the Territory.

I went through that country, myself, just after the soldiers had put these people out of their houses, and saw many families huddled around the still smoking embers of their burned houses. This act of vandalism, on the part of the Pro-Slavery, showing the subserviency of the party to the Slave Power. Later, the Osage settlers had been ordered to leave, and we were in daily fear of sharing a like fate to that of the settlers on those Cherokee lands. And I believe, but for the change of administration, such would have been our fate.

Thus, while all Nature seemed in a smiling mood, promising abundant crops, the year 1861 proved to be, us, one of the most trying in our experience.

CHAPTER 6

OF THE CIVIL WAR

The South, early began to show a determined aspect toward disrupting the Union, and in the event of war, we occupied a most unenviable position—with Missouri and Arkansas on our eastern border, and the Indian Territory on our south; our position in Southern Kansas, being peculiarly exposed to Indian raids, should they side with the south. It was not long before the firing on Ft. Sumter, and the call of the President for 75,000 men; and Kansas was responding promptly to the call.

It was proposed to raise one company in the South part of the county, and my brother and I conferred as to what we should do in the matter. We realized that we could not both enlist, leaving the family exposed as they would be to the raids from Missouri and the Indian Territory; we felt that it would be disastrous to our home interests, to remove the family and abandon our improvements, and it was determined that I should remain, and care, as well as possible, for the family and home, and he would enlist in the first company to organize in the county.

There was a company raised in and about Humboldt, with N. B. Blanton as Captain, and Samuel as First Lieutenant. This company was mustered into the Fourth Kansas, but later, it, with the Third, was mustered in as the Tenth Kansas Infantry.

During the summer, we were not molested, yet many rumors

were afloat, as to threatened invasions from Missouri and the Indian Territory. The Cherokees, Choctaws, Creeks, Chickasaws and Seminoles went off largely with the South, while the Osages remained loyal to the Government, and this fact, as to the Osages, was a great relief to our fears; as, if they were our friends, they would be a protection against raids from the unfriendly Indians. For our better protection, we organized ourselves into companies of Militia, and armed ourselves as well as we could. General Lane, was, during the latter part of the summer, busy organizing the Militia of the state, for its protection; the Militia of our county were under the command of Colonel Orlin Thurston, of Humboldt.

About the first of September, Ft. Scott was threatened with a raid, and Colonel Thurston was ordered there, with a portion of his command. Those in the South part of the county were left, as a protection to their homes. Before reaching Ft. Scott, the order was received to go to Barnesville, a point on the State Line, to act as picket guards, while the main force fortified a point about six miles back, which was called Ft. Lincoln, this point, General Lane designated as the "Key to Kansas." There, most of the men of Humboldt were holding the "Key," while a band of Rebels came in by "another door" and sacked their town. This was on the afternoon of September 8.

There was one company of Missourians, under Captain Livingston, and one of Cherokee and Osage Halfbreed Indians, under Captain Mathews. They passed about a mile East of us, on their way to Humboldt, and we did not know of their presence until after their departure. But few men were in Humboldt, and the town fell an easy prey to their hands; they did not kill anyone, but robbed the stores and private houses of such things as they could carry away. They hastened off, making a few calls on the way, as they returned South. On the following day as many of the settlers as were at home pushed after them with as much dispatch as was possible.

On reaching Lightning Creek, we were joined by a force of regular volunteer soldiers from Ft. Scott, under command of Col. Jas. G. Blunt, afterwards a Major General. We placed our force under his command, and we were led along down the Neosho river, hoping to find some of the Rebels at or about the residence of Captain Mathews. He was living on a fine ranch, just where the town of Oswego has since been built; he had a half-breed Osage Indian wife, and had a lot of fine horses and other stock. However, we found that he was not here, but had gone on further south, and that his men had scattered. This move, we were making in the night time, and with great caution, having with us a guide who was well acquainted with every trail, much of the way being through dense woods; passing on down the river, we obtained information that a part of the raiders were at the house of a Cherokee Indian, about three miles below where the town of Chetopa now is, and just over the line into the Indian Territory; we reached the place just about daybreak, and surrounded the house. Having discovered us, two of the occupants broke out into the bush and escaped; one, we took prisoner; Captain Mathews himself, with a double-barreled shotgun in his hands, ran out of the house and was shot down.

The one we captured was very badly scared; but on being satisfied that he had not been in the raid, he was discharged.

Captain Mathews was a man of influence among the Indians, and we had heard, during the summer, of him as having raised a company of Indians for the purpose of making a raid upon Humboldt, and settlements adjacent, and only awaiting a favorable opportunity to do so. This raid alarmed our people to such an extent, that many of our neighbors moved away; some going to the North part of the State, and some temporarily to Humboldt, or the North part of the county; those remaining, for the most part, left their houses at night, hiding out in the brush; but as for ourselves, we remained at our home, and never slept out of the house but one night. That night, just at dark, we were informed by a neighbor that a large force was seen passing east of us, in a northerly direction and, not being able to learn the facts in the matter, we thought it safer to sleep out. In the morning, we found the rumor arose from someone seeing a herd of Indian ponies grazing on the prairie.

The people of Humboldt now took extra precautions to prevent another raid. They kept one company of Infantry in town, and they were building a fortification around O'Brien's mill; and one company of cavalry was kept out, for most of the time, as scouts, in the direction of the Indian Territory.

On the 14th of October, this company of cavalry returned from a scout of several days to the south line of the state, reporting that no sign of rebels had been seen. This report quieted all fears, at the time, and the people were wholly off their guard when, later in the evening, a force of three or four hundred rebels, under Col. Talbot for Arkansas, of the Confederate Army, came dashing into the town and easily captured the place, taking most of the Militia force prisoners. One man, in attempting to get away on a mule, was shot and killed. Captain Livingston, who was with the former raid, was also in this party. After setting fire to nearly every house in town, and robbing them of such things as they could carry away, they liberated the prisoners and returned south with all possible dispatch, small detachments calling, as they went, on most of the settlers on their routes.

We learned of this raid upon Humboldt just about sundown, and we expected a visit from them on their return, probably some time during the night; and, from the fact that since the former raid, General Lane's forces had captured and burned Osceola, Missouri, and on the south line of the State, in Cherokee County, a reputed Southern sympathizer running a small store, had been robbed and murdered by some irresponsible persons claiming to be Union men; and, from the further fact of my own part in the pursuit of the former raiders and the killing of Mathews; I did not feel like trusting myself in their hands. And we therefore concluded to carry such things of value as we could, to some safer place, and secrete them among the rocks and timber on the bluff, near the lake; and also, to hide ourselves likewise.

We therefore gathered up our best articles of clothes and bedding, tying them up in bundles for carrying away. I also took a team of horses from the stable and tied them down under the bluff, in the dark; and we had not, as yet, carried out any of the bundles, when, just as the sun was setting, I looked out to the North, in the direction of Humboldt and saw three armed men riding up the slope towards the house. My first thought was of neighbors gathering for the purpose of following the rebels; but as they came nearer, I saw that they were strangers, and that they approached with arms at "present".

I saw, at once, that an attempt to escape was futile; and I determined to put on a bold front; and so, walked out to the gate in the rear of the house a distance of but a few steps from the door, where, at the time, my wife and two or three of the children were with me. My wife followed me out; I saw that they were half-breed Indians. I spoke to them as a settler to a stranger. One of them, as spokesman, proceeded to question me as follows:

"What is your name," this, I gave him.

"Are you armed, or have you arms in the house?" I said that I had no arms; but, in the house, was an old shotgun out of repair, and asked him very politely to alight and see for himself.

He asked if I had any horses. I told him that I had two ponies, but that they were running out.

He sent one of his men to the stable, and finding no horses there, seemed satisfied without a search in the brush.

He then asked me where I came from, and whether I was an abolitionist or a pro-Slavery man. I began to feel that such questions were vital, and calculated to draw me very close to the danger line; but whatever might be the result, I determined to make a true statement.

I said that I had come to Kansas from Indiana, and was naturally a free-state man; that I had come to make a home for my family, and that it was my desire to make Kansas a free state; but that I accorded the right of men from the South to settle here and make for themselves a home, and to establish slavery by fair means, if they could do so. We had considerable further conversation; and in answer to my questions as to why they were burning houses, and robbing people who were at their own homes and attending to their own business, disturbing no one, they gave no direct answer; but in excuse for raiding Humboldt, he said that they had learned that certain persons, who had been engaged in the murder and robbing of the store recently, in Cherokee County, were being harbored in Humboldt, and that they were seeking them.

I expressed a hope that success might crown their efforts, as I did not approve of such unlawful acts; and, at the same time, I suggested that it seemed to me that they were engaged in the same kind of business. I learned that they were Cherokee Indians. I will do them the credit to say that they did not respond harshly or use any harsh or profane language, in all our intercourse; and finally, they rode off without having dismounted, which, if they had done, and gone into the house on my "cordial" invitation, they would most likely have carried away a part of our ready-packed things.

We felt greatly relieved at their departures and on the morrow we learned that none of our neighbors had fared so well; in fact every other family along their route had left their homes and hidden out; so that, as the several squads visited these houses and found them abandoned, they carried away such things as they could, and destroyed most everything else.

This second raid was very discouraging to the settlers, in general, and many who had remained up to this time, now abandoned their homes and removed to points North and East.

In view of the exposed situation of the settlers along the southern border of the state, the Government placed a force of Volunteer soldiers at Humboldt; sometimes having one or more regiments stationed there; the building of a block-house was commenced but never completed. This gave us a feeling of greater safety from the Rebel raids.

Nov. 6, another son was born, we named him Oliver.

The winter 1861-2 was passed with any events of unusual interest.

In the Spring of 1862, several thousand Indians of the tribes of Creeks and Seminoles, mostly, having sided with the Union cause, were driven out of the Territory by the more numerous Rebel Indians.

They went into camp, with their families, near Neosho Falls and Leroy; and during that summer three regiments were organized among them for Government service, officered by white men.

The year was, for the most part, uneventful for us; we were undisturbed by the Rebels, and our lives were as peaceful as could be, under the circumstances; we were having no immigration to our part of the state; our settlement, in the two years passed, had considerably decreased.

In 1863 our condition remained much the same.

A force was kept at Humboldt most of the time; and under its protection we felt comparatively safe; we were having fairly good crops; on account of the war, everything we had to purchase was very high. Samuel had been promoted to the Captaincy of his company, and from him we received substantial aid towards living expenses and the improvements on, and the stocking of the farm.

In August, with others of the neighborhood, I was at the Sac and Fox Agency, where it was expected the Commissioner of Indian Affairs would meet with the Osage Indians to agree upon a treaty for the disposal of a portion of their lands.

I was there in the interest of those settlers who had gone upon their lands prior to that time to secure for them the right to purchase 160 acres, to include their improvements; as it was understood that Eastern parties were seeking to secure the entire tract at a nominal price. The unsettled condition of affairs in the State, however, prevented the coming of the Commissioner.

While there, on the early morning of the 21st, the murderous raid of Quantrill was made on Lawrence; hearing of which, I, with Colonel Thurston of Humboldt, started in a buggy to drive to the place, a distance of some twenty or more miles. The day was very warm, and when about half way there, the Colonel became so very sick that it was thought well to turn back.

I thus failed to see the result of one of the most barbarous butcheries that occurred during the entire Civil War.

The year of 1863 was rather uneventful in our lives, at our home. On the fifteenth of August, another daughter was born; we named her Alice.

Early in the year of 1864, we were called upon to meet our first great domestic sorrow, in the death of our first-born daughter, Cynthia. She was taken down with pneumonia. Our facilities for caring for her were not the best, house open, physician only such as the country at that time afforded, but we had seemingly gotten her beyond the crisis of the disease, with strong hopes of her recovery, when a very sudden change of the weather, with a strong cold wind, made it impossible to shield her from its effects; she was taken worse, and died on the twentieth of February, in her twelfth year.

She was a child of great promise; she had not enjoyed many advantages of education; but she had improved her opportunities to a wonderful degree for a child of her age; had developed a very bright and charming character, and her loss was deeply felt by her parents; and I can truly say that I think there has never since been a day that I have not felt her loss.

During this year, our Militia force was more thoroughly organized; six companies were formed in the county, and called the "Allen County Battalion", under command of Colonel Twiss, of Iola.

I was commissioned as its Major, by Governor Carney.

Three of these companies were raised in the north part of the county, and were under the immediate command of Colonel Twiss, while the other three were from the south part, and were under my command.

The Captains of the three companies in my end of the County were J. M. Moore, G. DeWitt, and D. C. Newman.

In the latter part of September, General Price, having made his celebrated raid north through Missouri, on his way south was threatening invasion of Kansas. General Curtis, being in command of the Department, issued an order proclaiming the state under Marshall Law, and ordering all male persons over the age of 16, and under 60, to be mustered into the service for the protection of the state from the threatened invasion. All the military force stationed at Humboldt was sent to the Front, exception a small squad of the 11th, Kansas, under command of Major Haas. All the militia of the lower Neosho valley were under command of Major Gen. J. B. Scott, of Leroy. The Allen Co. Battalion was ordered to Ft. Scott, but, in view of the defenseless condition of Humboldt, the companies under Captains Moore, DeWitt and Newman, were left at Humboldt under my command.

We went into camp, and ordered all persons able to bear arms to come into camp, also, and details were sent out to bring in any who were not prompt in reporting for duty.

It was amusing to see some suddenly become sick, and, in their minds, unable to perform service; but no excuse was accepted, all were brought in; and, if claiming to be ill, were turned over to Dr. Scott, who was Post Surgeon, for examination; when, in most cases, the Doctor decided that the exercise and the diet incident to the service would be beneficial to their health.

We made our camp in, and around, the incompleted block-house.

Captain Newman's company was placed down on Big Creek, to act as scouts in that direction. Major Haas, who was in command of the Volunteer force at the Post, was ordered to furnish rations for the Militia, which; for a time, he did; but finally refused to issue to Captain Newman's company, unless it was brought to Humboldt. In fact, he wanted to take command of the Militia, but this, the Militia resented as we were not ordered to report to him. We claimed to be under our own officers. The Commissary stores were kept in the Lutheran Church, in the East part of town, in charge of a sergeant.

The Major of Militia believing that he was in the right, and knowing that he possessed the might, determined to help himself.

He therefore made a requisition for five days rations for Captain Newman's company, and on the refusal of Major Haas to honor it, Captain Newman was directed to help himself, which he did, taking only the amount called for in the requisition, and receipting for it to the Sergeant in charge. Major Haas, thereupon, ordered both Captain Newman and myself under arrest, but, fortunately for us, he had no power to enforce his order. And so it seemed that a Major of Militia outranked a Major of Volunteers.

After the Militia were disbanded and at their homes, the Major sent a detail to the home of Captain Newman and took him under arrest to Humboldt; he was detained overnight, and discharged.

After remaining in camp at Humboldt some three weeks, we were ordered to Ft. Scott with two companies; Captain Newman's company remaining at Humboldt, also a squad of colored men under Captain Eli Gilbert. We left Humboldt about sundown, reaching Marmaton Creek about midnight, where we received orders to go to the Ft. Lincoln; we halted here until daylight. While here, the village of Marmaton, a few miles down the creek from our camp, was raided by a rebel band, sacked, and burned, and six persons killed. In the morning, we proceeded in the direction of Ft. Lincoln, but on reaching Raysville, we were ordered to Ft. Scott, arriving there a little before midnight.

We were marched out northeast, to a position occupied by Colonel

Twiss. Soon, it began to rain, and we were in a sorry plight to have met the enemy who was expected at any moment, and whose guns could be heard in the distance all night.

We put out a strong picket guard and the balance of the men; sought such rest as could be found; some, in the wagons we had along, and others, in fence corners or such places as afforded some shelter from the drizzling rain.

About the time that all was quiet, a signal gun was fired at the fort, and one of our men lying in a wagon, thinking that the enemy was upon us, jumped from the wagon, and, managing to get through our lines, made a bee-line for Humboldt, where he arrived during the next day, a run of fifty miles. He was a very good man, but frankly acknowledged that he was a coward, and insisted before starting that there was no use in taking him, as he could not fight.

The next day, Price's army, hard pressed south along the Missouri line, east of Ft. Scott, passed us. We did not see them but could hear the guns as the battle raged.

The only feat our men performed that day, worthy of note, was what we then called "a grand flank movement" of five or six miles up the Marmaton. The men were not to blame—and I do not know if the officers were. We were drawn up, in battle array, on the high prairie, north of Ft. Scott, early in the morning; the entire Militia force under Maj. Gen. Scott—of Leroy. He was present with his staff; after quite a wait, word was given out that the force in Ft. Scott had concluded to abandon the place, and fell back upon the village of Marmaton—some nine miles west; and just then, a body of men was seen approaching from the north, and they were supposed to be a portion of the rebel army; seemingly too great a force for us to withstand, and we were ordered to retreat in the direction of Marmaton—which we did, on the "double quick"—our Maj. Gen. and staff in the lead. We took a straight course, pulling down fences and crossing fields, when in our course. The story as to the abandonment of Ft. Scott, was incorrect; and it was soon learned that the approaching forces were friends, under Col. Moonlight, commencing a regiment of Kansas Volunteers; on learning which, we turned back to Ft. Scott, reaching there some time after nightfall, finding it full of Union Soldiers.

Gen. Pleasanton, with his command, was there, with about six hundred prisoners, among whom were the rebel Generals Cabel and Marmaduke.

The next day, we returned home, were soon thereafter, mustered out, and this was substantially the end of the war, with us.

During these years we had made some improvements on our home; had increased our cultivated land; had added considerably to our stock, both cattle and hogs. My brother had sent home something from his pay from time to time, and we were induced to make an investment in Texas cattle, with rather disastrous results.

With our neighbor, Wesley Garroutte, we bought two hundred two-year old heifers, for which we paid $1600.00—each of us paying $800.00. We got them in the Fall, in fair condition, and had plenty of feed to carry them through the winter; the winter was severe; they would not eat corn; they became thin, and before Spring, nine-tenths of them died. And such was the general result with all who undertook to handle Texas cattle. They were not used to being fed, and could not endure the cold of our winters. It is a strange fact—but true—that you might throw them out a wagon load of corn with the husk on, and they would eat off the husks and never eat one ear of the corn. I knew some men who, one fall, bought and brought into the neighborhood one thousand head of 4 and 5 year old Texas steers, in fine condition; and before Spring, they had less than 100 living cattle.

During the summer, I had built a concrete house about 16 x 30 feet, one-and-one half stories high, with cellar. Soon after moving into this house, a heavy rain storm came; and, the water not being carried away properly, ran down the walls and washed out a portion of them, and a large part of one side fell down, not having been very substantially built. However, the roof had not fallen in, and in a short time the damage was repaired, and we had a very comfortable house.

That fall, I was elected a member of the Legislature from the fifty-fourth representative district; it being the South half of Allen county—including both Iola and Humboldt; the North district sending J. A. Christy.

At this time, there was a great fight between Iola and Humboldt as to the County seat. The Democrats made no nomination.

J. McClure, of Iola—a Republican—made an "Independent" race against me; however I beat him, about three to one.

Dec. 27th, our little daughter Alice, about sixteen months old, died. She had been burned quite badly, but we had not looked for any serious results; but she took a severe cold, and that developed into pneumonia.

Samuel, on the 29th, at Monticello, Ill., married Miss Dolly Tinder; and bringing her home, they fitted up the small concrete house and lived in it.

In Jan. 1865, I met with the Legislature in Topeka. Jacob Stottler was elected speaker. The most important business was the election of a U. S. Senator. The selection of members in the Fall election hinged largely upon the question of "Lane" or "Anti-Lane."

And the Lane forces were largely in the ascendancy; consequently, the election resulted in the re-election of J. H. Lane, for the term of six years, to succeed himself. My seat was contested by Mr. McClure, on the grounds that I was not a resident of Allen County, for the reason that my residence was on the Osage Indian reservation.

It was a fight of Iola against Humboldt; there were no real grounds for such a contention, but it served the purpose of embarrassing me for about half the session; I was given the seat, in the end.

Some of the members of this Legislature afterwards attained to some prominence. Jas. M. Harvey, who sat next to me, became Governor of the state, and, later U. S. Senator. He was a man of fair ability, and unflinching integrity. Geo. W. Glick became Governor—the only Democrat ever so honored. He was afterwards appointed by Pres. Cleveland, U. S. Pension Agent. Cyrus Leland became a Republican leader in the state, and was, by Pres. McKinley, appointed U. S. Pension Agent; and he is, at this time, (1903) the recognized boss of the Republican machine, in Kansas politics.

Soon after the adjournment of this legislature, I received the appointment from Pres. Lincoln, as Register of the U. S. Land office, at Humboldt. This appointment, being made after the adjournment of Congress, would hold only until the close of the next Congress. The appointment came to me entirely unsolicited on my part; the office was not paying very much, at that time; J. C. Burnett was then holding the place; and wishing to engage in other more profitable business, he favored my appointment, and being close to both Senators Pomery and Lane, who were also my personal friends—I was favored without opposition.

I think that I took charge of the office in July; Dr. Geo A. Miller had been acting as clerk for Mr. Burnett, and I retained him in that capacity for two or three months, attending in person, two or three days each week. Afterwards, Jno. Francis acted as my clerk for several months. Late in the Fall, the business of the office becoming considerable, I bought the W. C. O'Brien residence in the southwest part of town, and removed my family to Humboldt.

In leaving the farm, I took two or three cows with me, leaving with my brother whatever else of stock and farm implements we had in common. While he was in the army he sent home such of his pay as he could spare, which was used in improving our home and in the purchase of stock, and in the expenses of our living; we had been together nearly ten years; and all our belongings, we had held in common; no account was kept between us, and no settlement has ever been made, nor was there ever any question between us, as to our individual rights. We did our business under the name of "Stewart Brothers."

CHAPTER 7
OF THE OSAGE TRIBE

The title to our land had not yet been obtained.

On the 29th of Sept. of this year, the Osages had made a treaty, under the provisions of which all settlers on their lands prior to that date, should have the privilege of entering 160 acres each, at $125 per acre.

And here, I enter upon a new period in my life; I had spent nearly ten years of my life in an attempt to make a home on a farm, under most unfavorable and trying conditions. Our settlement was upon unsurveyed land, which turned out to be Indian land; far away from towns, railroads, post office, schools or churches; during the early "border" troubles and the Civil war; we had been upon the very frontier of settlements, subject to constant raids from both rebel Whites and Indians; and just now we were beginning to feel a sense of security for self and home. Humboldt was beginning to recover, somewhat, from the effect of the rebel invasions, and just now fortune seemed to favor us as we took up our abode there.

And here seems to be a fitting place in which to speak more fully of a people, who, for several years of our life in Kansas, have figured very prominently in the same—The Osage Indians.

The Osage tribe of Indians was known as "blanket Indians". They owned a tract of land lying along the southern boundary of the state, fifty miles wide, North and South, by over two hundred East and West. A tract called the "Cherokee Neutral Lands" twenty five by fifty miles, joined them on the east, adjoining the state of Missouri.

The Osages formerly lived in Missouri, and by treaty in 1825, removed from there to their reservation, as described above. They were never considered a hostile tribe—it being a boast of theirs that they had never been at war with the United States.

At the time we first became acquainted with the tribe, it was said that it numbered five thousand. They subsisted, for the most part, by hunting at that time; they made two general hunts each year; going out far to the west, supplying themselves with Buffalo meat and hides. One hunt was made in the summer, for about two months time, in July, August and September. On this hunt, they saved the meat and tallow for food; the hides were not dressed for robes, as the hair was too short; the skins were used for covering their wigwams, and for other purposes.

Late in the fall, they made a second hunt, remaining all winter. On this hunt, the Buffalo were killed mostly for their hides, which were worked into robes for their own use and the market; these, when dressed, were exchanged with traders for flour, sugar, coffee, blankets and such other stuff as was used in making their clothing. The meat, they cut into long, thin strips, which were placed on a frame-work of poles, over a fire, and dried without salting. The tallow was fried out and put into the skin of the stomach of the buffalo. On the fall or winter hunt, they remained until grass was good, and in the spring when they returned with the meat and tallow packed and carried upon their ponies.

When going on a hunt, the entire family was taken along; the squaws to care for the meat and to dress the robes.

At home, they lived in groups as villages; sometimes several hundred in each village; each village had a "head man" or chief, who was recognized as the head of that community; while over the whole tribe there was a head chief.

When we first knew them, there was a village on "Village Creek", on the west side of the Neosho river, north of where Chanute is built. The chief of this village was called "Town Maker". Another village on the east side of the river, seven or eight miles south-east of us, had a chief named "Little Bear," and, He, I understood, was the chief of the "Little Osages." For there was a distinction between the "Great" and "Little" Osages—but I never learned in what the distinction existed.

Another village farther South, had a chief called "Strike-Ax". There were other chiefs whom I did not know personally.

A noted chief was "White-Hair", living down near the Catholic mission; and other, named "Chetopa" had lived farther south, but I think he had died before we came to Kansas. The town of "Chetopa" was named for him.

I became the most intimately acquainted with Little Bear, who was a frequent visitor at our house; and I esteemed him a true friend, and he, on more than one occasion, assisted us in recovering stolen property from the Indians. On one occasion, I had bought a pony from an Indian for $100.00; the very first night, it was stolen by the same fellow. On seeing Little Bear, a few days later, he promised that it would be returned. In a couple of days, the Indian brought it back. On another occasion, when the Indians had gone on their Fall hunt, I missed a gray horse we owned, and we had no doubt it had been taken on the hunt, and so the matter rested all winter; when, early in the Spring, before the Indians had generally returned, Little Bear came to the house, and I told him about the missing Horse. He at once said that he had seen the horse with the Indians—describing him better than I could, saying the Indian and the horse were on the Verdigris, and as soon as grass would do to travel on, they would come over, and the horse would be brought home; and, in due time, the horse was returned. He was not very valuable; he had been used as a pack horse, and was reduced in flesh; he had no doubt had a pretty hard time, and I think he was glad to get home.

Little Bear was a fine appearing man, of large physique, and I would have felt as safe under his protection as under that of any man.

I regarded him as a man of honor, sincere and honest; he died in the seventies, in a village near Neodesha, and was buried on the top of a high mound near that town.

When we first settled on our claim, my wife, her mother, and the children had never seen an Indian; and of course, for a time, were much alarmed on seeing them ride up to the house in full paint with tomahawk and jingling bells attached to their legs, and with their abrupt exclamation of "How! How!" would proceed to dismount and file into the house—sometimes in numbers of ten or twelve.

After a time, that natural fear gave way to curiosity to learn something of their ways and language. They were always hungry and we soon learned enough of their language to know that when they said "Wan-um-bra", they wanted something to eat; and we thought it policy, at least, to give them such as we had. The squaws were most persistent beggars, and it required the most constant watching, when they were about, to prevent them from carrying off such articles as they could put their hands on.

I do not, however, believe that all Indians will steal, as I found some whom I felt that I could trust fully. We had, especially, one old friend who seemed to fall very friendly toward us; he often visited us, sometimes with two or three squaws, who seemed to be his wives. Our little daughter, Cynthia, only four or five years old, grew to regard him very highly, and he would tell her their Indian names of things while she sat on his lap. The old Indian seemed to think a great deal of her, and would pull down her ears and show how they ought to be slit, so as to be ornamented with rings as the Indian girls wore them.

On one occasion, when the Indians went on their hunt, to be gone all winter, this old Indian and his squaws brought a quantity of their belongings, and stored them in our yard, near the house, for safekeeping while they were gone; on their return, they were pleased to find everything as it had been left.

As before stated, we did some trading with them, finding some profit in it; as we could do better with such goods as they wished than the money, in accruing buffalo robes or ponies. The usual price of the robes was $4.00 which we would dispose of in Kansas City at a small advance. The Osages did not dress their robes as well as some other tribes.

In the spring, the squaws put in some corn and pumpkins, in small patches near their villages, the ground being usually grubbed out in the bottom lands in the edge of the timber. The squaw did all the work, such as the planting and cultivation of the crops; the dressing and care of the game, and the building of wigwams.

A fire is built in the center of their wigwams, over which meat and vegetables are boiled in a large iron pot; meat is also broiled over the coals. Bread is baked in skillets, or is fried in the buffalo tallow in a kettle—much as we fry doughnuts. They usually boil, with their meat, pumpkins, beans and green corn; they dry the green corn, in the summer, in large quantities; also pumpkins for winter use. Their ways of handling and cooking their provisions are anything but cleanly; they waste no part of an animal that is killed. They will kill a beef, take off its hide, and at once, begin to cut up, cook and eat; stripping out intestines with the hands, and, without washing, cut them into strips, roast and eat. They devour the heart, liver, and lungs—so that nothing is lost; and a company of twenty or thirty Indians will eat an entire small-sized beef at one meal.

A very common feature of every village is the great number of dogs that will come out to meet you with much yelping; they seem to be a mongrel breed, of a cross between a dog and a wolf.

The Osages, on the death of one of their number, make a great outcry; wailing in a most hideous manner, for hours, and beating their tom-toms—a sort of drum made by stretching a skin over a hollowed out log.

The dead are usually buried on a high point of land, in a rough rock vault, mostly above the surface of the ground, with a covering of flat stones; the body is wrapped round with a blanket, and many trinkets are buried with the blanket. In the winter time when the ground is frozen, or covered with snow, they sometimes use a hollow tree, into which—at some distance from the ground—the body is placed. I found one such case, in the timber about a mile from our place, where, at about twenty feet from the ground, a hollow limb had been broken off, and in this, a body had been shoved, head first. I could see some parts of the blanket, with the feet, (apparently) sticking out.

Since our settlement, the Osages have greatly decreased in numbers, provided that their number was correctly given, as five thousand. At this time, 1904, the number is less than 1800. While they were poor then, they are reported to be the wealthiest people pro-rata, on earth. The sale of their reservation in Kansas, realizing for them over $8,000,000.00, which the government holds for them, and is paying in annuities, 5 per-cent per annum, besides they have a valuable reservation on which they reside in Oklahoma.

In conclusion, I can say for the Osages, that in the long time that we had lived upon their lands, we had but little cause to complain of their treatment of us. It is true, that as a rule, they would steal, and we had to guard against that tendency at all times; on the other hand, during all our trying times during the progress of the Civil War, we had never any fear of harm to person or property from them; but felt that they were a protec-tion in warding off the raids from the rebel white men of the South.

CHAPTER 8
OF POLITICS AND POETIC JUSTICE

The house I bought in Humboldt had been run as a hotel by O'Brien; it was indeed, the only one in town, and while there was much need of a hotel, it seemed hard to close it; and so, I became a hotel-keeper, perforce of circumstances.

We inherited, with the house, two or three regular boarders and cared for such travel as came to us; we, indeed did not solicit customers, but as far as possible, discouraged it; but in spite of all we could do, we were soon overcrowded with travel, as immigration began to turn to this area of Kansas.

About this time, a daily mail service was established between Lawrence and Humboldt, and a hack was put on, carrying the mail and passengers. This hack, with its passengers, stopped with us, and by the Spring of 1866, the house was greatly crowded, and that summer, I built a stone house adjoining and connected it with the old one, and my business grew beyond all calculations.

The business of the Land Office also increased to such an extent as to become a fairly good paying office.

January 18, of this year, another son was born to us, to whom we gave the name of Edwin.

Humboldt, since its partial destruction in 1861, by the rebels, up to this date, had made but little improvement. It now took on new life; the fact that the Osage Lands were soon to be opened up for settlement brought to this part of the state, many persons looking for homes on those lands, as well as many other looking for business openings; and Humboldt was the town located most conveniently to those lands.

There was also a large quantity of land subject to entry with land warrants and college Scrip, as well as under the Homestead Law, in the counties of Woodsman, Greenwood and Butler, at the Humboldt Land Office; all of which contributed to make the town a good business place.

Prior to this time, there was not a brick of stone building in the town; but this year, besides the stone house built by myself, there was the stone Catholic Church and a schoolhouse, and a brick block on the west side of the public square-used, for a time, as a hotel and saloon; also, several good frame buildings.

When Congress convened on March 3rd, President Johnson, who became President on the death of Mr. Lincoln, and whose policy I refused to support, would not send my name to the Senate for confirmation. Republicans in Kansas were generally opposed to the policy of Mr. Johnson; though Senator Lane supported him. But in coming home in June, and finding most of his party friends bitterly opposing the administration, he was so chagrined that, on July 1st, he shot himself with suicidal intent; and on the 11th, he died.

Mr. Pomeroy, our other Senator, was opposing Mr. Johnson, and could not consent to the appointment of other than a radical Republican and, so, Congress adjourned without the appointment of a Register being made, and after its adjournment, the office was closed.

In July, Col. Thurston, a Democrat, went to Washington and secured the appointment from the President. When Congress met, his name being sent to the Senate, he was rejected; Mr. Johnson then sent the name of John W. Scott, of Iola, a Republican, but seemingly not so obnoxious to the President as I; but he was promptly rejected, also.

It becoming apparent that some sort of a compromise would have to be made, the name of Col. N. S. Goss, of Neosho Falls, a Democrat, was sent in as Register, and that of D. B. Emmert, of Ft. Scott, a Republican, for Receiver; and the Senate confirmed them, and thus ended my first term as Register of the Land Office.

The office had become a good paying one, and I regretted this loss, especially so, as I had bought and improved property in Humboldt.

But by this time, I had found the hotel a very good paying concern.

The ousting of Col. Thurston gave me much satisfaction. And I was pleased that Col. Goss, a warm personal friend, had been given the place. When he took charge of the office, I went in with him, and helped him get hold of the business, as he was wholly unacquainted with the manner of doing the business.

I, at once, opened a real estate office, in connection with the business connected with land entries, giving attention to contest cases before the land office.

Col. Goss took charge of the office early in the spring of 1867.

Some time, during that year, S. S. Dickinson came to Humboldt; he was a young man, lately out of the army, and I took him into partnership, in the real estate business, under the firm name of "Stewart and Dickinson" and found him an honest, energetic, and capable man; well suited to the out-door business, while I did the office work.

At that time there were many persons from the East coming to the Land Office with College Scrip and Land Warrants, to locate upon Government land; and Mr. Dickinson took such parties out into the Western counties and made selections for them, and we charged them a fee of $5.00 for each quarter section. On some trips of several days, we would locate ten or more sections of land.

During this year, I made much more money than I could have made had I been the Registrar of the Land Office.

Mr. Dickinson was in business with me until 1869, and during all that time we did a very satisfactory business.

In September, last fall the "Rocky Mountain Locusts" of a better name, grasshoppers, visited this part of Kansas; and in such multitudes to darken the air, in their flight. When alighting on the fields of corn they stripped the stalks of all blades, in a few hours, and the ears of the green corn of their husks, and ate the soft corn to the cobs. As rapidly as possible, to save any feed, the corn was cut and put into shocks. As to fruit, they ate peaches, leaving only the stones hanging on the trees; apples, they did not eat, but ate all the leaves, leaving the apples hanging on the trees without the leaves to protect them from the hot sun. After destroying every green thing, they deposited millions of eggs in the ground, to hatch out in the next spring. As cold weather came on, they disappeared, seeming to die. In the spring of 1867, millions of eggs hatched, but the hoppers did not live to do any harm, as there came on a spell of cold, wet weather, which seemed to get away with them.

On the fourth of April, 1868, was born to us another daughter to whom we gave the name of Mary Ella.

In January of this year, I made an entry on 160 acres—our home place of "Cottage Grove." I made the first entry on the Osage lands, first of all of that land lying in the south part of the state, comprising a tract of 50 miles in width North and South, by over 200 miles in length, east and west. Samuel made entry No 2, Col. Goss, Registrar of the land office, accorded us that privilege, as being the oldest settlers on these lands. And thus, after nearly twelve years, since settlement upon our claims, without any title to the land, we secured the title of our home. This was under that clause in the treaty with the Indians, by which settlers prior to the date of treaty—September 29th, 1865—were entitled to purchase 160 acres, covering their improvements. Only about two or three hundred settlers were entitled to such privilege.

In the early spring of this year, 1868, a town company was formed for the purpose of locating a townsite at some point near the south line of the state, on the line of the proposed railroad then building down the Neosho river.

The company was composed of Dr. Geo. Lisle, Col. W. Doudna, Col. N. S. Goss, Dr. J. B. Torbert, Mr. John Secrest, Mr. Henson, and myself. We bought 320 acres of land, on which we laid out the town of Chetopa. The company made very liberal donations of lots to secure the building of a schoolhouse, several churches, a hotel, and several business enterprises.

We secured the railroad, now known as the Missouri, Kansas & Texas, the town built up rapidly, and before the close of the year we had one of the best towns in Southern Kansas.

At the election that fall, the Republicans elected General Grant President; and in the spring of 1869, Col. Goss, recognizing that "to the victors belong the spoils", decided to tender his resignation to the incoming administration; at the same time, intimating his desire that I should make application for re-appointment to the place. I had not thought seriously of such a thing; was doing very well in my own business and had not given much attention to politics for a couple of years; and it was pretty well understood over the state that P. B. Maxson, of Emporia, had been promised the place by Mr. Pomeroy, in consideration of services rendered him during the last Senatorial election. I had not looked on the office at that time as one of very great profit; but I could see that it would not be long before the Osage lands would be open for entry, at which time, as one sold through this office, the business would necessarily be very large.

I was also informed by Col. Goss that Mr. Maxson had accepted a position with the railroad Company then constructing a line of road from Junction City via Chetopa, through the Indian territory to Texas, and that he did not want the office.

On this assurance, soon after the meeting of Congress in March, I went to Washington, with a view of presenting my claims for the place.

Senator Pomeroy and Congressman S. A. Clarke had the control of the patronage in Kansas; the other Senator, Mr. Ross, being a "Johnson Republican" and without influence with the administration.

Both Pomeroy and Clarke were my friends, but both informed me of their obligations to Mr. Maxson. I assured them of my information that Mr. Maxson did not desire the place; they told me that they were not so informed by him, but that if I could secure his statement to that effect, they would gladly give me their support.

I therefore went to work to find him, using the telegraph; but had no success for several days. I finally located him in the Indian Territory. On finding him, he at once telegraphed to Senator Pomeroy his declination of the office. In the meantime, however, the President had sent in the name of Mr. Maxson; but on the receipt of Mr. Maxson's telegram, Mr. Pomeroy had his name withdrawn, and mine sent in.

The Senate at once confirmed the appointment, and I came home much elated; as a joint resolution was then pending in Congress, provided for the disposal of the Osage Ceded and Trust lands; and I knew its passage would assure a greatly increased business at the Land Office.

The resolution was passed on April 10, and the lands were opened for entry in July or August following.

My commission was issued, and signed by Gen. U. S. Grant, President; and on May 12th, I entered upon the discharge of the duties of the office. In connection with my appointment at this time, I felt the more gratification from the fact that my reappointment came to me as a Lawrence paper put it, "as an act of poetic justice."

I wish also to record my appreciation of the conduct of both Senator

Pomeroy and Congressman Clarke, in the matter. The Senator assured me at once that he was pledged to Mr. Maxson, and although he was not on the ground to press his claim, he proposed to act in good faith towards him. Much has been said against Mr. Pomeroy, as to his subsequent action, in offering Mr. York, a member of the Kansas Senate, a large sum of money for his vote for a re-election to the U. S. Senate; and, indeed, all the facts as developed in that case, are strongly against him. I have always felt there was a conspiracy among his enemies to put him in a false position. Certainly, in his connection with me, I can truly say that his every act was most honorable. I can also say the same for Mr. Clarke.

Senator Ross, the colleague of Mr. Pomeroy, had been a supporter of the Johnson Administration, and therefore had no influence with the Grant administration, and consequently could do nothing for me; although I had known him for a number of years, and he is my personal friend. Mr. Ross, by the way, was greatly maligned by the Republican Party, for his course on the trial for the impeachment of President Johnson; but I have always given him credit for honesty of purpose in that action. At the same time, it resulted in his political death in the state of Kansas.

CHAPTER 9
OF LEGALITIES AND FINALITIES

In taking the office of Registrar the second time, I found soon after the Osage Ceded and Trust lands open for entry; and a very large number of settlers, since the making of the treaty in 1865, had gone upon these lands, and were anxiously awaiting an opportunity to secure title to their homes; there was a very great rush of business in the office.

The land office had always charged certain fees for filing homestead and other entries, over and above the legal fees; these fees, being understood to be the prerequisite of the office to cover the expense of clerk hire; for which the Government made no provision.

I adopted the same rule; charging just such fees as had been established by my predecessors, no more, no less.

The business so increased that, in order to accommodate those applying for entry, I was compelled to employ two clerks, at an expense of nearly $200.00 per month; and it was our aim to collect sufficient of these fees to pay this extra expense; this seemed altogether satisfactory to our customers. But as the business increased, certain attorneys asked the office to permit them to make out the necessary proof papers for the entry man, allowing them to charge the usual fee, which they proceeded to divide with the office. We refused to make out any proof papers on the plea of lack of time. On our refusal to make such an arrangement, these attorneys undertook to make us trouble with the Department, as well as with the settlers.

A couple of young attorneys by name of J. M. Balderson and L. W. Keplinger, had recently come to Humboldt, and they were induced to undertake to work up a case, and bring a suit, against the officers, on a charge of extorting certain illegal fees from the entrymen; and in order to secure a basis for such a suit, they went among the settlers and represented that we had charged illegal fees, and in such cases as they could accrue an assignment of their claim, for a nominal sum, they took such assignments, until they amounted to about $4,000.00—for which sum suit was brought in the District court. Our attorneys filed a demurrer, on which the case went to the Supreme court, where the demurrer was sustained by the concurrence of the entire court; in consequence, the case was thrown out of court, with costs on them!

They also succeeded in securing our indictment in the U. S. Court, we never attended the court, but our attorneys had the indictment quashed. The cost of defending, in these suits, was very considerable; and the harassment of mind was much more serious; its tendency was to create a more or less antagonistic feeling among the settlers, which was most unpleasant to us. It was, however, some satisfaction to us, to know that the parties never realized a cent for the time and money spent in the prosecution of these cases, and had all the court costs to pay.

Mr. Balderson soon after left Humboldt, locating in Wichita; Mr. Keplinger, later, went to Kansas City, Kansas, where he has succeeded in building up a good law practice. He afterwards freely expressed his regret at having had anything to do in the matter, and had shown himself on more than one occasion—my very cordial friend.

Indeed, the whole affair was instigated by Col. Thurston, and one H. C. Whitney, on the part of Col. Thurston, from his personal spite at me, for supplanting him in the office of Registrar, and my refusal to make terms with him for dividing the fees; and Mr. Whitney was simply his tool.

Notwithstanding these suits were in our favor, I think we made a mistake in not conforming strictly to the letter of the law; yet such a course would have resulted in greatly delaying the business of the office, and in subjecting applicants for entries to much more expense in awaiting their turn in the ordinary course of the business of the office; as the Government would not allow us compensation for clerk hire, or if we had hired clerks, as we did, to facilitate the business, and paid them out of our salaries and commissions, we would have but little left for ourselves. The course we pursued, at the time, seemed to us the best for the parties doing business with the office, and for ourselves.

As it was, the business of the office during 1869, 70 & 71, in the disposal of the Osage lands, was very great; the sales amounting to over $1,000,000.00, for which the Government paid me only about $500.00.

Immigration to this part of the state was very large, and the Hotel was doing a good business. I was unable to give it much attention, and I secured James Brady, an Irishman, to act as clerk and manager, and he proved to be the right man for the place; he was thoroughly honest, and wholly devoted to my interests, at the same time, he was considerate of the comfort of the guests.

During these years, I made money as rapidly as I could desire; Humboldt was on a boom; I invested money in many things.

I was in a company that built a toll bridge over the Neosho river, and was also in a building association which put up a number of houses for rent, and rent was very high.

I think that in 1870, I bought the Pogue farm of 130 acres in the bottom adjoining the 160 acres that I already owned; also bought from Mrs. Amos, 120 acres, lying South, and running up on the hill to the east. This

I bought with the view of having high ground for a building site, as all my other land was lying in the bottoms.

In 1870, in connection with J. B. Torbert and S. S. Dickinson, I traded land for some flouring mill machinery in Illinois, and brought it out to Humboldt, putting it into the stone mill which we had built on Cole Creek, about a mile south of town. I owned an equal interest with Torbert and Dickinson. We had a good many thousand dollars in this enterprise, which proved to be a bad investment. I gave no personal attention to the mill business, and in the end lost all I had in it.

That year, in April, the M. K. & T. Railroad was completed into Humboldt. To secure the road, the citizens were required to purchase 160 acres of land on the west side of the river, to be laid out as an addition to Humboldt, through which the right of way should be given the road, ten acres for depot grounds, and one half the balance to be given to the railroad company. A few of us organized a company, and paid $13,000.00 for the site, $1,000.00 of which I paid.

In the month of November, the town celebrated the completion of the L. L. & G. Railroad as far south as Humboldt.

All these things gave to Humboldt a real boom, and I thought we were to have the principal city of Southern Kansas.

Some eastern parties, stopping with me for a few days, conceived the idea that the hotel business was about the best thing in sight, and offered to rent my house, furnished as it stood, agreeing to pay me one hundred dollars per month for one year.

I had already commenced building a residence with the intention of quitting the hotel business, and this offer seemed too good that I accepted it, and we at once moved to a small house until our own could be completed. I had secured a whole block on one of the nicest locations on the town site, and when the house was completed with barn, etc, the cost of the property was about five thousand dollars. We moved into this house in the fall of this year, 1870, furnishing it throughout with new furniture.

Our furnishings, however, were not complete until the next spring, when my wife and I bought a lot of carpets and lace window curtains in St. Louis.

Humboldt, was at this time, enjoying unbounded prosperity. It had two railroads and was expecting to get an East and West road from Ft. Scott to Wichita. It had the U. S. Land Office, which brought to it a great number of the settlers from the south and southwest counties, and the course of filing upon, and making entries of their land.

Congress had provided for the sale of the balance of the Osage Lands, known as the diminished reserve lands; and those lands were settling up very rapidly. The two years limit for the sale of the Osage ceded and trust lands, expired April 10, 1871, and the diminished reserve lands were open for entry in the July following.

During the partial lull in business of my office, in May 1871, my wife and I made a visit to our old home in Lafayette, Indiana and also to Troy, Ohio near which place I was born.

We had a most enjoyable visit by our old home place in Lafayette. After an absence of fifteen years, we found, however, many changes in the place and people. Many of the cherished friends of our early married life were gone, some to other parts of the country, others to the bourne from which no traveler returns.

In my old home in Ohio, the place of my birth, but few of the friends of my school days were to be found.

On returning home, I found that on the opening of the new lands, there was unprecedented rush for entries at the office.

I think that within the month of July our business was at its maximum. The sales amounted to about one hundred thousand dollars, and the ensuing two or three months, only slightly less. In the meantime, the bulk of the business came from the counties lying south and southwest of Humboldt. Many settlers having to come the distance of from fifty to one hundred miles. An effort was being made to remove the office to some more central point. Independence and Neodesha were making strong efforts to secure the office. Humboldt put up a vigorous fight to retain it, but in the end, was ordered removed to Independence, and I was directed to go to that place by the Commissioner of the General Office, and secure office rooms for its use, which I did and in November the office was removed.

I had become so identified at Humboldt that I resigned the office of Registrar, and on the 20th of November, my connection with it terminated.

This was the turning point for Humboldt. The railroads were pushed on south, good towns were built upon their lands, according place of trades for the peoples of the counties in the south and southwest, the east and west road was diverted to run via Iola, and the loss of the land in itself was a very material one.

Travel and trade fell away rapidly, and values of property declined greatly, the parties to whom I had leased the hotel, after a few months, could not afford to pay such a price as had been agreed upon, and I reduced the rent to twenty five dollars a month.

In 1868, Reverend James Lewis came through Humboldt, and organized a Presbyterian Church. He was very popular as a man, had served in the Civil War as a Colonel of the New York Regiment, and he was better known as Colonel Lewis, than as Reverend Lewis. He boarded with us quite a while before his marriage, and became somewhat as one of the family. We attended his church and the children were in that Sunday School.

In 1872 or 1873, my wife and four of our boys, united with the Presbyterian Church, under Mr. Lewis's administration. I was not in full accord with them in my belief, and my early education had tended to fix in my mind, a prejudice against this church, but I can say that since the time I connected with the Presbyterian Church, my relation with its people has been most pleasant.

Sometime before this, I had become a member of the Masonic order.

During these years, 1873, I was more or less connected with the city government as one of its councilmen, and was also a member of the school board.

After resigning the office of Registrar, I gave some attention to land contest cases before the land office, and though I had never studied law, under the taking of testimony before the office, I was able to hold my own with some of the best attorneys of the district. My knowledge of the land laws giving me some advantage over most attorneys in these cases.

On May 11th, 1872, another son was born and we named him Arthur.

During these years, from 1871 to 1874, but little occurred in my life of interest. I was giving some attention to the farm which I rented but from it not much was realized. My holdings in Humboldt had greatly depreciated in value, and all over the country, values had also decreased.

On the 24th of August, 1874, our only remaining daughter, Mary Ella passed away in the seventh year of her age. It seemed like the life of our home had gone out. She was a bright and happy child, and I have never said that it was all for the best. It has always seemed like it was an evil to have her life with us cut off in her early childhood. It seems like it would have been better if she had developed into a life of happiness and usefulness here. A life of happiness to herself, and usefulness to her friends and the world. We were situated in such a way as to give her the best of medical aid, and the most loving care, but the disease of typhoid claimed her as its victim, in spite of our efforts to retain her with us, her life was transformed to the spirit plane, where I believe she still lives, and develops to a higher life, and that still, she cares and helps her friends on this earthly plane.

Our seventh son was born November 20th, 1875, and we named him Allen.

The grasshoppers visited us again in the fall of 1875, and in the spring of 1876, the eggs laid in the fall hatched in great numbers, and the young hoppers did much damage, especially along the streams in the bottom lands. I had a field of some thirty acres of wheat that was looking very fine, but as the young hoppers reached it in the movement they were making toward the east, they ate it up in a day, and the corn, as it came through the ground, was eaten off from day to day until it was destroyed.

In June, we replanted the corn, the hoppers having died or flown away and we raised a fair crop.

Looking around for something to do, I concluded to try the loaning of money for eastern parties, more especially to settlers on the Osage ceded lands, which under the Supreme Court decision were soon to be opened for entry at the land office.

These lands were in the counties of Neosho, Labette, and Wilson, and in the fall of 1876, I started out on horseback and took application for loans, meeting with very good success.

When these lands were opened for entry in the spring of 1877, I went to Independence and opened an office as a general real estate and loan agent, and also gave attention to contests between the land offices.

I succeeded in building up a very good business, in a very short time adding fire insurance to the rest. My family in the meantime remained in Humboldt.

I had Joseph, my son with me for some time, and later, when he went into business at Humboldt, Ollie came with me for a time.

In 1880, in company with my Sons Frank and Fred, in August, we went to Colorado. We went on the Santa Fe to Pueblo, thence over the Denver and Rio Grande to Colorado Springs. We went to Manitou, where we got a tent and small camp outfit, and pitched our tent on the fountain creek. A short distance above where Ruxton flowed into it, where at that time, there were no buildings, Manitou being then a very small village. There was some sort of a building about the soda springs, a bath house, but none at the iron springs.

We explored, on foot, many places of interest, looking upon the

Garden of the Gods, visiting Williams Canyon, the Ute Pass, and Rainbow Falls, Crystal Park, South Cheyenne Canon with its Seven Falls, etc.

On the tenth of August, I think, we started in the early morning to make the ascent of Pikes Peak on foot, there was no trail road at that time. We went by the burro trail. The distance of fourteen miles, from Manitou to the top of the peak, which we made by about 1:00 P.M. was a toilsome walk, but I stood it as well as the boys, being never conscious of no discomfort from the great altitude of over fourteen thousand feet.

I was quite cold, some snow on the trail near the top, but the view from the top was magnificent beyond conception, and it well repays anyone for any discomfort experienced in the ascent.

We sent a telegram to the home folks from the top, the Government maintaining a signal service station there.

After an hour or two of rest, we started on our return, reaching camp about 6:00 P.M. pretty well worn out, but after taking a soda water bath and a hot supper, we slept well, and in the morning felt all right. Our entire trip was one of great interest and pleasure never to be forgotten, it was my first; I have made two since.

My business was successful beyond my expectations. I had a good real estate, loan and insurance business. Joe having gone into business at Humboldt, I was left alone in the office.

A young attorney by the name of J. M. Thompson, was doing something as a pension attorney in connection with his law business. He seemed an energetic young man, and I took him into partnership in the loan and insurance business, retaining as my part, the real estate, and he the law and pension part, and he and I operating together only in the loan and insurance business. Our firm name was that of Stewart and Thompson.

This was in the spring of 1881. We thought that we ought to get money for loaning direct from the parties in the east, instead of through loan companies in the west, and in August, I made a trip east for the purpose, if possible, of interesting eastern capital in western securities. I visited Boston, Hartford, New York, Philadelphia and Westchester in the quest, but was unsuccessful.

On my trip, I stopped over a day in Chicago, from there I went over the Grand Trunk road via Battle Creek, Lansing, and Flint, Michigan. Crossing the Detroit River at Fort Huron into Canada, and passed through Stratford and Guelph, Toronto, and Lake Ontario and Montreal crossing the St. Lawrence River on the Victoria Bridge, two miles long at St Albans, into Vermont, then through Waterbury, crossing the Connecticut river into New Hampshire, passing through Concord, Franklin to Boston, where I spent two days, visiting various places of interest, as the Navy Yard, Bunker Hill Monument, the State House, Colonial Hall and the Commons.

I then went to Hartford, stopping off a day and visiting the races at Chester Oak Park, where the trotting horse Humboldt, won the trotting in two-twenty the miles, and little Brown Jug made a mile pacing in two eleven and three fourths, the fastest time made to that date by any horse. Jaude S. was to have trotted, but was lame so as to be unable to do so. She had made the best time on record at that date, but I don't remember the time.

I went on through New Haven by rail, and there took Steamer to New York. This was a very enjoyable ride, down Long Island Sound a ride of about five hours on the briny deep.

I went immediately to Philadelphia, where I stopped a day, visited Fairmount Park, where the Centennial fair was held five years before. After going to Westchester, I returned to New York, where I stopped a day and visited Central Park, and the old Trinity Church, climbing to the top of its steeple, 280 feet high, from which a fine view of the city was had. The next, I took a steamer for Long Branch, the great summer resort, had a fine view of the mighty ocean, and took a bath in its water.

Returning from New York, I came via the B. & O. to Chicago and then to Kansas City.

I think that Mr. Thompson, was with me about two years, when, in a business transaction of his own, he appropriated some funds collected for a client, and on being hard pressed, he skipped out of the country. The firm was not involved in the transaction, but he left in my debt about one hundred dollars, part of which I secured by taking a buggy and some books for it. I did well enough to get rid of him on as easy terms as this, as I found that he was reckless in his expenditures, and his word was not to be depended upon.

After he left me, Ollie came down and remained with me for from one to two years, when he left me to accept a position with Moses Neil, at the Sac and Fox Indian Agency. He had been appointed by President Cleveland during his first term as agent for those Indians.

In 1884, I bought a tract of about five acres, in Holeman's addition to the city of Independence, and built a neat cottage at a cost of about eighteen thousand dollars for a lot and garden, and in the summer I moved my family there to reside.

Fred and family also came to Independence to live, with a view of assisting me in my business. He afterwards built a house on about two acres of the land I had bought. When the Missouri Pacific was built to Independence, he was appointed as its agent, and later he had accepted an agency with the Rock Island and moved away from Independence.

I improved our place by setting out fruit, and small fruits, and cultivating a nice vegetable garden, so that we had a very pleasant home place. My business has been fairly successful, and my standing in the city and county was good.

I transferred my membership with that of my wife, to the Presbyterian Church of Independence; also my membership in the Masonic lodge.

I was a member of the school board for a number of years, and one of the Trustees of the Presbyterian church.

I was situated favorably for the enjoyment of life, my only drawback was the failing health of my wife; she was much afflicted by rheumatism, and we did not seem able to secure any remedy at all effectual for her relief. In the later eighties and early nineties, times became hard in money matters. The Populist party was crying "Calamity", until parties in the east declined to loan money in our country; and mortgages were foreclosed. Immigration fell off, greatly; altogether, these things affected my business disastrously.

My son Arthur was married in 1892, and left home, and soon after, Allan left us to take a position in the First National Bank in Parsons, Kansas. Thus, my wife and I were left alone; her health became so poor that much of my time was required at home to care for her, which greatly interrupted my attention to business.

Both Oliver and Allan were living in Parsons, Allan was there, young and without a home. My business was not paying, and on the solicitation of both Oliver and Allan, I sold out in Independence, and in the fall of 1894, we removed to Parsons.

I very reluctantly consented to make this move, as it was a financial loss, in the disposal, at that time, of the property of which I was possessed. Besides, our home place, I owned with Mr. W. T. Yoe, a farm of 640 acres on Fawn Creek—with incumbrance of $1,000.00. It was reasonably worth $10,000.00, but could not be sold just then at any price; and as Mr. Yoe had advanced some interest payments on the mortgage, I deeded the farm to him, taking a bond for a deed, on condition that I would, within two years, repay him the amount advanced, and any further amount he would be required to pay upon it in the meantime.

But I never was able to comply with the conditions; any time after four or five years, my half interest would have brought me from $2,000.00 to $3,000.00 over the incumbrance. My residence property was also fairly worth $1,000.00 more than I realized in the disposal of it at the time. Both these properties were acquired at conservative prices, but all property was greatly depreciated in values, at that time.

Allan rented a house for us, and made his home with us. I did not engage in any kind of business.

In the Spring of 1895, my wife and I went to Washington D. C. to visit with our son Joseph and family. While there, my wife, when walking through a store where there was a step down, made a misstep, and, falling strained one of her ankles, from which she was laid up for over a month before we could return home, and could walk then only with crutches for long thereafter.

Soon after returning from Washington, my wife had a paralytic stroke, from which she never fully recovered. The paralysis was on her right side, somewhat affecting her speech, and, in a measure, her mind. However, she so far recovered as to be able to walk about and do some work about the house.

In December, Allan was married, and continued to live with us, for a time.

About this time, Ollie and family removed to Humboldt. In the spring of 1896, my wife and I visited our son, Arthur, and family, in St. Louis at the time of the meeting of the National Republican Convention, which nominated William McKinley as president; I was privileged to attend several of the sessions of that Convention.

In the summer of 1897, we removed to Kansas City; rented up-stairs rooms, living there about six months. In the meantime, the health of my wife had so much improved that I thought I would return to Kansas and again engage in business. I thought favorably of our old home place, Humboldt. But after looking over the ground, I decided upon Erie, where, late in the fall of 1897, we took up our residence, renting a small house with a large gardenpat (sic) and quite an orchard of apple trees. I rented an office, and opened up as a Real Estate and Loan Agent, with fair prospects as to business.

My wife seemed to have, in a large measure, recovered from the effects of her paralytic stroke. However, during the spring of 1898, she and I were returning home from church, when she made a misstep by reason of a defective sidewalk, and fell on her face, bruising her face considerably, and no doubt jarring her brain badly.

On the second night thereafter, she had another stroke, after which she was never able to walk, or turn herself in bed.

She continued in this helpless condition for more than a year. I procured a wheel-chair, in which during pleasant weather, I placed her, and wheeled her about the town; and sometimes would call upon a neighbor, all of which, she enjoyed very much. Late in the fall, I took her, with a nurse, to visit with her son Fred and family, in Washington, Iowa. I returned home, expecting her to remain for a month or more; but in a few days she became very anxious to get home and she returned.

I was compelled to give her the most of my time, in consequence of which, my business was neglected.

During the season of 1899, I made garden, as usual, my wife continuing in the same helpless condition.

I had a nurse with her all the time, and the neighbor women were most kind and helpful through all her illness. She was, considering the long period of her helplessness, quite cheerful and patient; such comfort and loving care possible to be given, was cheerfully accorded her by husband and absent children, and her loving appreciation was constantly shown.

On the 28th of May, 1899, at about the noon hour, she quietly and peacefully passed into the better life, leaving a husband, seven sons, and seven daughters-in-law, besides numerous other relatives and personal friends to mourn her loss. She was in her sixty-seventh year. She had been a sharer of my joys and sorrows, as my wife, for more than forty seven years; a loving and faithful wife; a kind and tender mother.

She was a domestic woman, caring more for her family than for society. In my earlier life, I had felt very keenly the loss of our three daughters, but in this bereavement, I have experienced the crowning sorrow of my life, and yet, I grieve not "As without hope." I live in the full confidence that her real self still lives, and that she cares for me, and is much with me even now, and that she is happy in the society of her children and others with her.

And when I shall pass into that life, I shall find her and our children, waiting to welcome me to that blissful state, where we may ever be together. After the internment of the body, in the Humboldt cemetery, I returned to Erie and disposed of most of the furniture. I went to Washington, Iowa to make my home with my son Fred and family.

Here I brought such things as were necessary to furnish a room for myself, and with them I have since had my home, in Washington, until the fall of 1901; and since that time, in Davenport.

CHAPTER 10
OF TRAVELS AND THE FUTURE

For about two months in the winter of 1899-1900, I visited with the family of my son Joseph, in Washington, D. C., and enjoyed the trip very much.

In 1901, and the summer of 1902, I did some work in an effort to secure persons for the "Homeseekers" Excursions, on the "Rock Island" to Southern Kansas, Oklahoma and Texas. I made several trips which afforded me an opportunity of seeing these countries at very little expense, with no financial profit to me.

But it gave me something to do, the time was well spent.

In August, 1900, I went with Fred and family, and several others friends, to Colorado. We had a large tent, and camped out for nearly six weeks. We camped on the Ruxton Creek, about one-fourth mile up it from Iron Ute Springs, but there is a great change—the surroundings new, as compared with twenty years ago. The old peak is there, much the same, also other mountains and canyons, but Manitou has made great changes, and Cog Railway is running to the top of the peak.

I visited all the places of interest, seen twenty years before, but I desired to walk to the top again, so one evening I started in company with my granddaughter, Mary, and Homer and Mabel Crawford, friends from Washington, Iowa, all born since I had made the trip first in 1880.

We started at eight P.M. with the purpose of reaching the summit before sunrise. On reaching a point about half way up, about two miles beyond which was known as "Half-Way House", we fell in with a gentleman and his wife, and two young ladies, with whom we kept in company for most part of the way to the top, which we reached just as the sun began to climb the eastern sky. During the night, we had kept up a slow but steady gait, stopping about midnight to make a cup of coffee and to eat our lunch.

We had some rain on the way. On reaching the summit, my hat rim was frozen, as was also, my beard icy. I sat quite exhausted, and exclaimed, "Glory Hallelujah."

I was congratulated by the man running the restaurant as the oldest man he had known to make the ascent on foot.

We went into the house, and had a cup of hot, strong coffee, and soon felt refreshed, when, after a couple of hours, spent in looking at the wondrous views presented to our visions, we started on our return, reaching camp about 4:00 PM. We were camped close to the line of the Cog Road, and we walked upon its tracks on our trip.

The winters of 1901 and 1902, I spent at Washington, D. C., with my son Joe and his family. My business in Washington was an effort to induce Congress to provide for the payment of a claim made by former registrars and receivers of land offices in Kansas, for the sale of the Osage Indian Lands. My brother Samuel was with me part of both winters, and we finally succeeded in securing an act of Congress referring these claims for adjudication to the Court of Claims.

These claims arose from the sales made of these lands, from the time I was in office, 1869 to 1871, to the present time, and the amount of claim in the aggregate in about $150,000.00 dollars.

Suit for my own claim was filed in the court, March 20, 1903, and is now pending.

Again, in August 1903, with my son, Fred, family and others, number-ing about twenty in all, including my brother Samuel, his wife and daugh-ters, Hattie and Effie, I made a trip to Colorado. This time we pitched our tents in North Cheyenne Canyon, about nine miles up the route of the Shortline Railroad, from Colorado Springs to Cripple Creek.

Location was ideal, within easy distance of all points of interest in and around Colorado Springs, and Manitou, all of which scenery had be-come familiar to me, but nonetheless interesting.

I made the trip over the Midland, as far as twin lakes, within eighteen miles to Leadville, and over the shortline to Cripple Creek.

The scenery along both routes must be seen to be appreciated. It is charming and picturesque beyond my ability to describe.

About a month was spent in a most enjoyable way when we returned home. On this trip, I did not essay to climb Pikes Peak, but nine of our party made the ascent one night.

And now I am drawing near the close of my sketch, possibly, near that of my life. I have endeavored to confine my narrative to my early life, and more especially, to my pioneer life and the frontier settlement of Kansas, passing lightly over my later life.

I am now passing my declining years at the quiet home of my son. Making frequent visits with the families of my sons and other friends in Washington, D. C. and St. Louis, South McAllister, and Kansas and Kansas City.

One son, Frank, is in California. Should I live, I hope to be with him ere long.

Sometimes, when in a reminiscent mood, I look back over the period of my life, contemplate all the improvements that have been made in all departments of life, within my own memory.

I wonder if it is possible that a like advance will be made during the present century.

I think that I never saw a railroad before I was twenty years old. We traveled by stagecoach, and in the part of Ohio where I lived, we had the canal built—from Cincinnati to Toledo—when I was about fourteen years of age. I rode on the first boat making a trip on that canal from Troy to Piqua, in 1840.

The steamboats were in use on the Ohio and Mississippi rivers, but I never saw one before I was twenty years of age. There were no ocean steamers, and a trip from New York to Liverpool required about five or six weeks' time.

It took a week or two to get mail from Eastern coast cities, and news from Europe was nearly two months in reaching us.

A letter coming five hundred miles or more cost twenty-five cents postage.

We had no telegraph. I was seventeen years old when the first telegraph message was sent, over a line from Washington to Baltimore in 1844.

The honor of formulating the message was accorded Miss Ellsworth daughter of the then commissioner of the patents, H. L. Ellsworth, of whom in after years, in Lafayette, Indiana, his home, I became well acquainted; also knew the daughter by sight. This was the message:

"What hath God wrought?"

Telephone communication, and all the present uses of electricity came in later.

Of course, we had no electric lights, and in only the larger cities were gas lights used.

During all my earlier years, we used tallow and lard lamps in our homes.

Churches, and public halls, were lighted with candles. The usual way of announcing a night meeting was to say: "Meeting at early candle lighting." Kerosene oil had not then been discovered, we had no matches with which to light the candles or with which to start fires. If we let the fire go out, we had to go to the neighbors for fire, or use the flint and steel to strike a spark.

In my early days, there were no cook stoves. Cooking was done over an open fire in an open fireplace. Our folks bought the first cook stove that I ever saw, when I was about ten years old, and it was the wonder and envy of the entire neighborhood.

There were but few manufacturers in the country, of any kind. We shipped to England our cotton and surplus wool, and brought back the manufactured goods. But our women for the most part, spun the wool and flax and wove it into cloth, from which the clothing for the family was made, as also were blankets and sheets.

The hides of our cattle were tanned in some nearby tannery, and our boots and shoes were made by the village shoemaker.

Very great improvement has been made during our lives, adding largely to the convenience, comfort and luxury of life.

I believe we have also made equal advances in religion, and spiritual life, as well as morals.

Now, after "looking backward" and seeing the wonderful progress made up to the present time, what may we expect as to the future?

Will the world make equally great advances during the next century? I think that we may reasonably expect even greater.

We have only made advances in material things, as we have learned more of Nature's laws, and have adjusted our lives in conformity to the same.

I think it not unreasonable to predict that in the future, as mankind becomes better informed as to the laws that govern the universe, of which we are citizens, they may be able to control the forces of Nature as to devastating floods, so far controlling the rainfall as to bring it within the requisites of the growth of vegetation.

In the understanding of Nature's laws, we are able to transmit messages through space, and it is claimed, by some scientists, that thought may be communicated from one person to another, without reference to distance.

Aerial navigation is measurably a success, and will, I DOUBT not, soon be in general use.

Is it visionary to think it possible that, as man becomes better acquainted with the laws governing the universe, he may be able to converse with inhabitants, if any there are, of other worlds? May we not, at least, hold communication with inhabitants of sister planets, revolving around a common center.

I think we can scarcely predict too much for the advancement of our race.

We have made great progress in material things, and are now entering upon a period of great spiritual advancement.

I feel sure that many of the inequalities now existing in society will be remedied; and our entire competitive worldliness will be superceded by some equitable system of righteousness, and, sometime all will come to recognize the divinity of God and the brotherhood of men.

Speed the day!

Finis

Acknowledgements

First and foremost, I'd like to thank Watson Stewart. This is his story, and I am forever grateful to have a hand in carrying on his tradition. Thank you, also, to the most important Stewarts in my life—Leslie, Ponna, and Alex.

I'd also like to thank my wife, Melanie, for her constant encouragement and my son, Wesley—the newest member of this family line—whom we welcomed into the world during my work on this project.

An immense word of gratitude, as well, for the crack team of folks that assisted in the creation of this book. Charlie Ray—my incredible narrator who brought Watson to life in the audio recording, Katarina Naskovski—who blew me away with an incredible cover design, and Bodie Dykstra—editor extraordinaire who formatted this book and was critical in maintaining an unaltered historical document.

And of course, I would also like to thank you, the reader. Thank you for choosing this book and embarking on the fascinating tale of Watson Stewart. It would mean the world to me if you would leave a review or share this book with a friend.

Last but not least, please remember that everyone has a story worth sharing. I hope to someday read yours.

Thank you.

www.ingramcontent.com/pod-product-compliance
Lightning Source LLC
Chambersburg PA
CBHW020410130626
46549CB00006B/2503